Now WHAT?

Now What?

© 2016 by Rachel Dawn

Unless otherwise noted, Scripture quotations are taken from the Holy Bible, New International Version®, NIV®. Copyright © 1973, 1978, 1984, 2011 by Biblica, Inc.® Used by permission of Zondervan. All rights reserved worldwide. www.zondervan.com. The "NIV" and "New International Version" are trademarks registered in the United States Patent and Trademark Office by Biblica, Inc.®

Scripture quotations marked esv are taken from the ESV® Bible (The Holy Bible, English Standard Version®). Copyright © 2001 by Crossway, a publishing ministry of Good News Publishers. Used by permission. All rights reserved.

Scripture quotations marked NKJV are taken from the New King James Version®. © 1982 by Thomas Nelson. Used by permission. All rights reserved.

Scripture quotations marked AMP are taken from the Amplified® Bible. Copyright © 1954, 1958, 1962, 1964, 1965, 1987 by The Lockman Foundation. Used by permission. (www.Lockman.org)

Scripture quotations marked GNT are taken from the Good News Translation in Today's English Version—Second Edition. Copyright 1992 by American Bible Society. Used by permission.

Scripture quotations marked NASB are taken from New American Standard Bible®. Copyright © 1960, 1962, 1963, 1968, 1971, 1972, 1973, 1975, 1977, 1995 by The Lockman Foundation. Used by permission. (www.Lockman.org)

Scripture quotations marked NLT are taken from the *Holy Bible*, New Living Translation. © 1996, 2004, 2007, 2013 by Tyndale House Foundation. Used by permission of Tyndale House Publishers, Inc., Carol Stream, Illinois 60188. All rights reserved.

Image Copyright Info:
Cover Image: Copyright: http://www.123rf.com/profile_stokkete'>stokkete/123RF Stock Photo
Chapter 1 Typewriter Image: Copyright: http://www.123rf.com/profile_michaklootwijk'>michaklootwijk/123RF Stock Photo
Glass slipper image: Copyright: http://www.123rf.com/profile_dazdraperma'>dazdraperma/123RF Stock Photo
Little girl with plane: Copyright: http://www.123rf.com/profile_choreograph'>choreograph/123RFStock Photo
Pottery Image in Chapter 4: Morty Bachar, Lakeside Pottery Studio

Advanced Praise for

"Now WHAT?"

A Story of Broken Dreams
and the God Who Restores Them

Could not put it down....

"I could not put this book down and **I wish I had a resource like this after my divorce**."

- Connie (Remarried, Columbus, OH)

This book is a must read....

"This book is a must read, for anyone who has ever felt abandoned or hopeless. The author shows a genuine and vulnerable side of herself and her story. I believe, no matter your own situation, you can and will, benefit from this book. My story is a bit different that the authors, but after reading this, for the first time in my life I feel like I'm not alone, I can hope and that with God's help, my future will be better than I could've ever imagined.

I stayed up till 3am and finished the book in one night. I loved every page. I laughed so hard at some parts I woke my daughter up! I keep thinking, when I have a hard copy, I'm going to go through so many highlighters!"

- Rebekah (Single Mom from Tampa, FL)

An engaging, easy to read story...

"'Now What?' is an engaging, easy to read story, that is relatable to everyone. Rachel Dawns voice is audible on the pages. **Solid advice for anyone fresh off of a divorce** and still applicable for those happily married. I would recommend this to anyone looking to improve their circumstances."

– Susie (Happily Remarried from Cincinnati, OH)

Real and honest...

I thought I knew about what it takes to have a great marriage, but after reading Rachel Dawn's book Now What, I was challenged to check some of my beliefs and expectations. **What I loved most about this book was how real and honest Rachel Dawn was with her own story and experiences!** I truly was able to learn from her mistakes AND revelations. Rachel Dawn's example of overcoming faith is a great testimony for anyone going through marital or life situations.

- Gaynelle (Happily Married from Cincinnati, OH)

Now WHAT?

A Story of
Broken Dreams
and the
God Who
Restores Them

Rachel Dawn

Contents

Foreword

It's been said that we are all either heading towards a crisis, in a crisis, or just coming out of a crisis.

Around about the time a beautiful, young woman named Rachel Dawn was being shoved headfirst into her own unforeseen marital crisis, I was finally seeing the light at the end of my own. While she was belting out psychedelic Santana lyrics and dancing naked on her bed with a bottle of wine (oh yeah, you really need to read this book!), I was uncovering the latest, best version of myself and stepping out on my first book tour with wobbly knees and a vision to change the world. As she was being gutted, I was being elevated to some of the most-prominent stages in the country to share a message of hope and purpose that had ironically come from the place of my greatest pain.

Neither of us knew the other, nor did we have any idea where our respective crises' would take us—or that they would bring us together for such a time as this.

In my travels, God had strategically orchestrated some connections that brought me to the Kentucky International Convention Center to speak into the lives of thousands of sharp, motivated entrepreneurs at their company's annual leadership convention. From the stage that day, I shared a statement that has become my truth, my life's mantra and the topic of every talk I have ever given over the past two decades: "God can turn your pain into purpose; your misery into ministry; and your heartaches into a heartbeat for others if you'll let Him". Little did I know, Rachel was a part of that audience.

A broken, hurting, twenty-five year-old divorcee at the time, Rachel was at her lowest of lows; but apparently, she was also more than ready to get up and move on. Like the true champion she is, she decided to put on her big-girl panties and start herself on a journey of restoration. She labored tirelessly with the Lord to get free of the shame, the regret, and the burden of unforgiveness that she'd been carrying for too long. And she never gave up. She chose to believe that God could do just what I spoke of on stage that day. No matter the cost, Rachel Dawn was determined to turn her pain into purpose, her misery into ministry, and the heartaches of her life into a newfound heartbeat to help others who find themselves in the same desperate predicament.

And she has.

Now What? A Story of Broken Dreams and the God Who Restores Them is the fruit of Rachel's intense labor to find hope amongst the shards of her broken dreams and a brilliant reminder that we are never alone. It's a reminder to keep pressing forward, to never give up, to square our shoulders and to confidently believe in a God who is faithful regardless of what our eyes and our hearts tell us. It reminds us that despite the darkness of our circumstance, there is a God who can still be found who never leaves us, nor forsakes us, and who never wastes a hurt.

And we all need that.

Rachel Dawn has since become one of my dearest friends. She'll tell you in this book how much I have taught her but let me assure you—she has taught me equally as much in the way of grace. I'm truly blessed and honored that God chose to cross our paths and align our hearts in this life.

It is my prayer that you will take a seat in your most comfortable chair and open your heart to receive from this mighty woman of God. Rachel undoubtedly knows what it is to be prancing one moment through a field of sweet dreams-come true, and then be blown to smithereens by a land-mine of betrayal and offense. By God's grace, she's successfully navigated her way through the devastation and despair. And thankfully for us, by God's great provision, we now get to hold her roadmap in our hands to discover for ourselves just how (and what) to get out of our own unique messes!

Whether you are heading towards a crisis, in a very real crisis at this present moment, or just coming out of a recent crisis, I truly believe and pray that the words on these pages will help you find solace in your searching and bring purpose from your pain—for it is only from that place of peace that the "Now What?" moments of life aren't nearly as scary, make the most sense, and yield the greatest rewards.

Jennifer Beckham

Co-Pastor of Restore Church and Author of *Get Over Yourself: 7 Principles to Get Over Your Past and On with Your Purpose*

Jacksonville, FL

Dedication

To Jennifer Beckham

Without your friendship, encouragement, guidance, and mentorship, these words never would have made it to the page, much less into the hands they are in now. Thank you for believing in me when I struggled to believe in myself, and for affirming I had a story to tell that people needed to hear.

To my husband, Barry

Thank you for loving me even when I am unlovable—which is a lot. Thank you for believing in me and pushing me to keep this project going in the times I felt discouraged or inadequate for the task at hand.

To Mrs. Franks

I have always been a storyteller. The idea and desire to do something with those stories was planted in my heart by my third-grade teacher, Mrs. Franks. After reading a short story I had written, she told me, "You have such a strong voice in your writing. You should be an author one day!" She probably told every third grader that, but to me it was prophetic!

Mrs. Franks, thank you for lighting a spark in this young storyteller to use her creative talents. For believing that I could and causing me to believe that about myself. And most of all, for showing me a living example of what a few words can do to positively impact someone's heart and mind for a lifetime.

To the one whose dreams have fallen all apart

And all you're left with is a tired and broken heart

I can tell by your eyes you think you're on your own

But you're not alone

Have you heard of the One who can calm the raging seas

Give sight to the blind, pull the lame up to their feet

With a love so strong it never lets you go

No you're not alone

— "Safe" by Phil Wickham[1]

Definition of a

"Now WHAT?"

Moment

"Now What?" Moment [nou wuht moh-m*uh*nt]

Noun: An event, or sequence of events, that culminates into asking oneself and life, "Now what?" usually out loud. The very lowest point of your life. The moment when everything you believed in comes crashing down around you, the trajectory of your future jolts to a halt, and you are left looking at the shattered pieces of your dreams wondering if life will ever look like the picture you had in your mind again. "Now What?" moments are often accompanied by feelings of lostness or hopelessness.

See also: Rock bottom.

Introduction

A Letter From Me to You

I wholeheartedly believe that Jehovah God, the Creator of the universe and the Lover of my soul, implored—no, *commanded*—me to write this book. I'm not arrogant enough to think I have everything figured out or got all the words right, but my heart has been in the right place of obedience to His directive to get my story on paper.

After following all of the rules, being the "good girl" and meeting and marrying my Prince Charming in true fairy-tale fashion, I found myself divorced, disheartened, and disenchanted by the time I was twenty-five. "Now what?" I cried out to *whoever* was listening, because I wasn't so confident there even was a God anymore. After all, I played by His rules and I still lost—big-time.

Have you ever found yourself in a place like this?

A place where you watched everything you ever believed crumble in front of you?

Watched your dreams wither up and die?

Questioned how there could be a God who loves you if you're hurting this much? Or wondered where He was when things were falling apart? When the doctor called? When the divorce papers came? When the judge's gavel rapped the podium?

Have you felt hopeless?

Confused?

Directionless?

Abandoned?

Alone?

Like the bad apple? Certain it would be better for everyone if you just weren't around?

If you've had any or all of these thoughts and feelings, let me assure you first and foremost, *you are not alone.* Over the last five years, God has taken me on a journey showing me who He really is—and isn't—and what that means in my everyday life.

This book is not just a story about a mid-twenties divorcée. It's about all of us who have experienced some kind of failure or dead-end, some shattering of our hopes and dreams, when we have looked around and asked "Now What?"

During this journey, God brought people into my life who have found themselves in their own "Now What?" moments - from prison sentences, to medical conditions, to military rejection. And He's given me the privilege of telling their stories in Part 2 of this book.

But first, let me tell you my story.

Even if you haven't been married or gone through a divorce, I want to encourage you to keep reading. I promise you that there will be truths about God's love and lessons to be learned from my journey that you will be able to relate to.

I'd prefer to be talking to you over dinner or a cup of coffee, but I can't do that with each and every person I believe this story will touch. So I hope you'll curl up with this book, and know that I wish I was there with you, sharing in your pain and comforting you with the parts of my story that would bring you the most hope about your own situation.

Jennifer Beckham, former Disney princess, now minister, author, and public speaker, said God once told her, "As long as your story keeps leading them to My story, keep telling it." *Okay, Lord, I hear You, so here I am telling it, one more time.*

My prayer is that you feel the hand and voice and love of the Father clearly and intimately as you read.

He wants to show up in your life too.
Let Him.
I promise, it's worth it.

Part One

My Story

The Beginning

It was a warm day in May 2006. I was waiting outside a train station in downtown Chicago with my best friend contemplating what we could do during the two hours we had to kill before our train came. We were the only two people standing outside the station other than a young uniformed sailor who was leaning covertly in the corner smoking a cigarette. *Ugh! I hate smoking!*

"Excuse me," I said, walking toward him. "Do you know any good restaurants around here?"

"Actually, I haven't been in town that long and I don't, I'm sorry."

"It's okay." I shrugged and walked away.

He threw down his cigarette, jogged to the curb, and hailed a cab. We watched as he leaned in and spoke with the driver, curious when he didn't get in but instead returned to where we were standing. The sailor announced he had the location and walking directions to a Greek restaurant three blocks away. "I'm waiting on my train too," he said very formally. "If you'd like, I can escort you ladies there."

While we walked, we talked about his short career in the Navy, my business trip to the city, our shopping that day . . . He was interesting. We also realized we'd all be taking the same train back out of the city. We were enjoying his company so much we even discussed meeting up for shopping the next day.

The sailor requested one check for our food; when I offered to pay, he looked at me as if I were speaking a foreign language and slid his card to the waiter. We walked back to the train station and boarded it together. The hour-long train ride abruptly came to end when the sailor jumped up, surprised. "This is my stop!"

Quickly hugging my friend and I, he turned and disappeared. Suddenly, a white uniform came rushing back up the aisle, grabbed my phone, and frantically typed in his number.

The next day my friend and I went to the mall, but when I tried calling the sailor, the number was invalid. At first we thought he might have given us the wrong number intentionally, but that just didn't make sense.

I spent the next couple weeks calling the naval base, searching online directories, and doing everything short of phoning the President to find this kid. I didn't want him to think we took his dinner and ran – all I wanted to do was thank him for the crab cakes!

Almost a month had passed when I got a phone call from my cousin who was also stationed at the base in Chicago. As a last-ditch effort, I had sent the pictures we took on the train to him in hopes that out of the thirteen thousand sailors on base, somehow he might know *our* sailor. As it turned out, the two of them had just met the very weekend before he got my e-mail. He told me our sailor's name was Alex and gave me his number.

I immediately texted a message to the number: "Next time you want to put your number in a hot chick's phone on a train, make sure you type the right number."

Within minutes my phone rang and a familiar stranger's voice was on the line. We talked.

We talked a lot over the next couple weeks. That Fourth of July weekend, he took a bus from Chicago to Cincinnati, and my best friend and I picked him up at the Greyhound station. We showed him all our favorite parts of the city, we took him to my parents' farm in Kentucky and went fishing in the dark, we all went to the drive-in theater, we let fireworks off in the middle of a field somewhere off Beechmont Avenue, and we danced in that field to techno music. And when he kissed me for the first time that night, I cried. It was a bizarre reaction, but something stirred inside me I had never felt with any other kiss in my life to that point.

On the last night he was in town, while we were lying in the grass, admiring the stars, cuddled under a blanket together, when he thought I was sleeping, he whispered in my ear that he loved me. That was the weekend I fell in love with him, although I still didn't even admit it to myself for a few more weeks and a couple more visits from him.

It sounds like a fairy tale, doesn't it? I mean, who doesn't want to tell her grandkids the story of how she met Grandpa at a train station in downtown Chicago when she was twenty-one? And how a whirlwind romance led to them eloping five months later?

Unfortunately, that was not the end of my story. Hold on, grandkids, things are about to get ugly, because real life isn't a fairytale. Wait . . . that sounds cynical, and that's not what this is about.

By the end of this book, I hope you come to the realization with me that life *can* be a fairy tale, but it doesn't just happen, you have to work at it, every single day. And sometimes other people still decide to walk out of your story because they are out of your control—and that hurts—but that's not the end either. By the closing chapter of your life, *everything* will have worked out in your favor if you trust His promise that it will.

Chapter Two

"We have tomorrows
for a reason."

The End

"Everybody's got a plan until they get punched in the mouth."
—Mike Tyson

I came home from work that Tuesday with the innate feeling that something wasn't quite right. I walked down the hallway of my little apartment and opened the office door. The room (where my husband had been sleeping the last few months) had been emptied. A quick glance around the rest of the small space revealed things missing from every other room as well. Then I saw it, the note on my kitchen table. In unfamiliar handwriting was a response to the list I had left my husband of things we needed to sort out prior to our moving to separate locations in the coming weeks . . . signed by his girlfriend.

Time stopped, though space started spinning. I pulled out my cell phone, speed-dialed his number, and heard, "The number you are trying to reach is unavailable at this time . . ." And it hit me: *He's blocked my number.*

The boy who had answered my text four years earlier after our chance meeting at a train station in Chicago. The boy I had married five months after that meeting. The boy I had shared the last four years and four homes with. The boy who vowed to spend the rest of his life loving me. The boy I had argued with almost every day in those last four years. The boy with whom I had gone through a year of marriage counseling. The boy who had called me at work, multiple times a day, "just to talk" not two weeks earlier. The boy who looked at me and spoke to me with contempt since finding this new person had blocked my number so he didn't have to talk to me anymore.

How could he do that to me? Not just leave, but let another woman come into *my* house and disrespect me like this? Who had I been living with for the last four years?

> "The Lord is close to the brokenhearted; He rescues those whose spirits are crushed."
>
> - Psalm 34:18 NLT

I collapsed to the floor like Jell-O released from a mold. My chest heaved with sobs I couldn't catch my breath fast enough to keep up with. I trembled and rocked myself until the streams of tears finally held back enough to allow my mouth to open again.

I called my boss to tell him I would not be coming to the office on Wednesday.

I called my mother-in-law, who cried with me and told me she did not raise her son to treat a woman that way.

I called the apartment office and had them come change the locks.

I called my father to ask him to be at my house the next day with his truck and trailer to move my things.

And finally, I called Alex's sister, who spent the next hour on the phone with me as emotional support. She understood everything I was going through. She bashed him and I drank. She made me laugh and listened while I cried.

I downed an entire bottle of wine and ended the night dancing naked on my bed to Santana.

The next morning I awoke with nothing left but angry grit and a firm resolve. I packed my entire life room by room. Everything of his that he had left I neatly stacked on the back porch, including his laundry in the dryer. I carefully folded every piece of it and left it there. *Kill him with kindness*, I thought.

Friends came and helped my father load everything up and within forty-eight hours I left that place, and that moment, behind.

Nine months later I received the documents that signaled the official end of my marriage. And three months after that I sat in the hallway of a courtroom as I waited for my last name to be called as "Kabuss" for the very last time.

Oh, and did I mention he brought *her* with him? And her fake boobs. And he never even looked me in the eye. We were in and out in less than five minutes, and with the judge's signature on the documents, the fairy tale for which I had waited my entire life ended.

Chapter Three

"For a seed to achieve it's greatest expression,
it must come completely undone. The shell cracks,
its insides come out and everything changes.
To someone who doesn't understand growth,
it would look like complete destruction."

— *Cynthia Occelli*

Now What?

Here I was twenty-five years old, divorced, broken, dam-
aged goods. Who would want me now?

I figured that by the time I got over the emotional turmoil,
found someone new, spent the acceptable amount of time dating
him, got engaged and remarried, I'd be in my thirties! And
surely my new somebody would be *way* below my typical dating
standards because what decent guy dates a divorcée? I know I
had advised all my guy friends against it. "They have too much
baggage," I'd warned. "They are train wrecks. There's obviously
a reason they couldn't stay married the first time. You don't
want to deal with that. Run away."

Now I was the train wreck.

How the *hell* did this happen? I was the good girl. I followed
all the rules, I waited for "the one" God had created for me, I was
a virgin until my wedding night . . . I did what I was supposed to
and it turned out like this?

If I followed God's plan and still ended up in the gutter,
where was God? Was there even really a God at all? Or was He
just as make-believe as Cinderella's fairy godmother? My clock
had struck the midnight hour, and I watched everything I had
ever believed in unravel before my eyes. These, and many other
tumultuous thoughts, were running on a continuous loop
through my head (more on that in chapter 4).

For now, though, you're probably wondering what went
wrong between the Beginning and the End. A lot of those details
aren't important, but I will tell you the parts of the story that
matter.

September 2006

Four months from the day we met, Alex and I got engaged. That weekend we came very close to having premarital sexual intercourse. After talking it over, we mutually decided to take a "fast" from one another. No contact whatsoever—no calls, no texts, no e-mail—for three days. We would pray and study during that time to see if God had really "chosen us" for each other. After the three days, we would come back together and decide if we were going to move forward and get married or go our separate ways.

At the time, it really seemed Alex and I were on the same page spiritually. Although he was not raised with as much of a spiritual foundation as I had been, he had become fairly devout while he was in the Navy. He had developed an extremely close relationship with the chaplain on his base and met with him almost daily as a spiritual mentor and guide.

On the third day of our fast, I read in a Christian publication the story of God calling Abraham to sacrifice his son Isaac and the spiritual lessons we can learn from that event. It was Abraham's obedience God wanted, not his son's life, and once God saw Abraham's full commitment to the unimaginable task, He spared the boy.

I was convinced (at the time) I heard right then in my mind and in my spirit that God was telling me that because I was *willing* to give Alex up, I could keep him. That scripture, along with the lyrics of Mariah Carey's "Butterfly" *("If you should return to me, we truly were meant to be, so spread your wings and fly Butterfly."* Yes, it's funny now, but that really happened.), flooded my mind with unquestionable assurance.

Our first conversation after our fast was tear-filled and joyous. When I told him about the confirmation I had received, he told me that he had just read that story in the Bible for the first time that weekend! What more confirmation did we need? We secretly eloped two weeks later in October and planned to have our formal wedding the following summer.

It was years later that I read, "Satan uses all kinds of things to speak to and deceive people—including scripture." And Mariah Carey songs, I guess.

They Say the First Year Is the Hardest

Three months after our marriage, Alex confessed to me that everything he had told me about what he believed in and wanted out of life, what his interests and values were, details of his past

relationships and his life growing up, basically everything about him as a person, was a lie, an act, to get me to like him. He became who he needed to be to get me to marry him.

Wait. Mr. Disney did *not* tell this part of the story.

While Alex cried and confessed all these things to me, I held him. Then I took a deep breath and did what I thought any good Christian woman would do. I told Alex I completely understood and forgave him for every bit of it. I told him I appreciated him making himself vulnerable and being honest with me now, and assured him we could move forward from that point with nothing else to hide, being completely honest with one another.

But even after our heart-to-heart, we still began to argue EVERY day.

Because *honestly*, he was a nineteen-year-old kid living in a new city, with a new wife, no friends, no job (because he had gotten out of the Navy early to be with me), and *no* idea how to be married (his parents had both been married three times at that point). And he blamed me for *all* of those things.

After a very short period of time, Alex just stopped trying.

Stopped caring. In hindsight, I realize his behavior was just as much a defense mechanism against me, his nagging wife, as it was his own apathy. But I wouldn't figure that out until *way* later. At the time, I was certain *he* was the problem and *he* was the one who needed to change.

I had been reading relationship and marriage books since I was sixteen, so by the time I met Alex, I felt confident and qualified to be married. I was an expert in my mind. I've since realized that reading those books not only didn't help me but probably actually hindered me. Not because of the books themselves, but because of the mind-set I had while reading them. I was setting up unrealistic expectations and creating an image of a perfect mate, perpetuating that delusion in my mind.

I used the things I learned from the books as weapons against Alex. "This book says a good husband does this and is more like this." I pointed out all the ways he didn't measure up and wasn't doing things the right way. And because I felt he wasn't holding up his end of the bargain, I thought I was justified in reacting the way that I did - disgustingly.

Hope Shattered

About a year into my marriage, my sister-in-law called me crying. She asked me to call my parents and have them come and get my brother's stuff—she had reached her breaking point and was kicking him out. They had been married for seven years.

Since the time they met when I was sixteen, this woman had been the big-sister figure I never had. She taught me how to dress, how to shop, how to wear my impossibly curly hair . . . And in my first tumultuous year of marriage I told myself over and over, *If she and my brother can keep their marriage together, I can make mine work.* I had seen some of their rough patches and knew about some of their struggles.

That phone call was a faith-shattering moment. As much as I

wanted to tell myself I could continue on and be the standard-bearer for our family in this area, I really didn't believe it. I lost a lot of hope that day.

And that was my own fault. Shame on me for basing my belief on someone else's actions instead of on a mountain-moving God. How immature.

The Unraveling

All three and a half years of my marriage were filled with verbal abuse and physical altercations. Alex was a master manipulator and liar. I became a person I was disgusted by. I never knew I was capable of such anger and venomous hatred. Words came out of my mouth I had never even thought before. Our relationship was toxic.

> I loved you
> at your
> darkest.
>
> Romans 5:8

He told me I was crazy and selfish so much that I started to believe both. When we would argue he would ask me, "What's wrong with you?" so often I started to think there *was* something wrong with me.

Eventually we both shut down.

All I wanted was to feel like Alex *wanted* to be with me. To fight for me. To be worth the effort. I had never been as lonely in my life single as I was in my marriage. I had more than one emotional affair with other men and I constantly fantasized about what life would be like if I hadn't married "the wrong person." Toward the end, I was so desperate to be out and starting over, there was even one guy I was going to run away to Italy with so we could start over together.

Alex and I went through a year of Christian marriage counseling, but counseling only works when both people are actually participating in the advice and following the directions of the counselor. Alex would make changes for a day or two, but then go right back to his old patterns and behavior.

I tried guilting him, threatening him, belittling him, challenging him, counseling him, and loving him into loving me. Nothing worked. He just went right on not trying, not caring, running away, and fighting. I eventually figured out that he started fights with me because if we were fighting, then he could justify doing whatever he wanted to do. Classic manipulation. And I let myself be sucked in every time.

A Whisper of Grace

One night Alex came home very late *and very drunk* after hanging out with his coworkers. After he stumbled into bed, I sat on the couch and prayed, *crying* to God, "How could he do something like that? Something he absolutely knows I abhor? How could he not care at all about hurting me or disappointing me?"

Yeah, it sucks, doesn't it? was the reply I heard in my head.

Ouch.

> *"When you're tempted to lose patience with someone, think how patient God has been with you all the time."*
>
> *- Anonymous*

It wasn't condemnation God was speaking to me; it was conviction. My memory showed me a quick reel of all the things I had done in my life that I knew God didn't approve of. But He still loved me anyway.

God showed me very clearly that night that when you love someone, you act in accordance with what they want; you sacrifice your own desires and pleasures simply *because* you love them.

It was the first time I understood how being a Christian really works, how genuine love really works. You don't just do something or not do something because you're *supposed to*, like I had all my life. You do it because you love God and you love the person, and you can't imagine hurting or disappointing them by doing anything else.

After that revelation, I felt so unworthy and overwhelmed by the way God still loves and pursues me even when I mess up and rebel. And I was flooded with an overwhelming sense of grace and compassion for Alex. I forgave him immediately and asked God to forgive me for being so hypocritical.

When Human Grace Isn't Enough

I learned to forgive Alex for a lot of things, but in the end it wasn't enough. He wouldn't forgive me for the things I had done (which, honestly, was quite a bit), and he still left.

I learned a lot in those four years about myself, about other people, and about relationships.

My marriage was terrible and messy and painful and depressing and lonely. But I wouldn't be who I am today if I hadn't gone through it. I would have been just as ill-prepared for my second marriage if I hadn't experienced all that crap.

We grow the most when we go through trials in life. "We can rejoice, too, when we run into problems and trials, for we know that they help us develop endurance" (Romans 5:3 NLT). Rejoicing probably wasn't my first response, but I got there eventually. How we respond in these situations shapes the very essence of who we are. Our character is forged in the rough tides, not in smooth sailing. Without the trials, as Paul called them, we would be very boring, weak, spiritually immature people. Not to mention, ill-equipped to help others.

The biggest lesson I learned through the last year of my marriage is that you can't control anybody. Ever. Not for the long-term anyway. Sure, you might guilt or manipulate someone into changing for a season, but it won't last and they will only resent you for it. The only thing you can control—ever—is yourself: your actions and your attitude, your reactions to the way other people treat you. And that's a full-time job in itself!

Other Things I Learned in 2009

On New Year's Day 2010, I sat down and penned a few other things I learned that past year:

Sometimes despite all your best efforts, cautions, standards, and tenacity, you just get hurt.

Sometimes you just have to let people go.

Sometimes you end up hurting those you love most.

Sometimes you simply screw up and miss it all together. And in those times, when you absolutely don't think you can get any lower or screw up any more, you find grace. And realize that it's all going to be okay.

Sometimes you have to let people in, despite how vulnerable that makes you feel. Because in the end they will help you grow, making you a better person.

Sometimes you discover things about yourself you never knew. Some of those things you may not like. Others you may be pleasantly surprised by.

God always knows best.

God brings people and experiences into our lives right when we need them.

Sometimes making new friends is exactly what you need.

Sometimes reconnecting with old best friends is the only thing you need. And when you do, it's the best feeling in the world.

Sometimes your circumstances—usually the ones you don't like—are absolutely no one's fault but your own. And you just have to deal with them, learn from them, and avoid them again in the future.

Sometimes you just need to slow down, take a deep breath, and start over. Maybe even tomorrow.

Sometimes you just need to take a nap!

Disciplined is not something that you are or you aren't. It's a daily battle to be disciplined, and it is determined by the decisions you make and the actions you take.

The same is true for everything about you in life. You are not who you think you are or who you believe you are; you are only the decisions you make, every day.

Which brings me to my next point: you can only lie to yourself for so long.

The good news about that is you can be someone completely different from who you are today just by making different decisions tomorrow. You can be exactly who you want to be.

Sometimes that's a relief, because you don't like who you are today. And if you do like who you are today, all you have to do is make those same quality decisions tomorrow.

Sometimes—no, all of the time—other people's actions are completely out of your control. The sooner you realize that and let that go, the easier life becomes. Even if their actions and decisions hurt you in the meantime.

Because sometimes despite all your best efforts, cautions, standards, and tenacity, you just get hurt.

A good laugh and a long sleep are the
two best cures for anything.

Irish Proverb

Chapter Four

He is with you when your faith is dead
And you can't even get out of bed
Or your husband doesn't kiss you anymore
He is with you when your baby's gone
And your house is still
And your hearts are stone
Crying "God what'd you do that for?"
He is with you.

—*Mandisa²*

The Fallout—Life After Divorce

"I wanted a perfect ending. Now I've learned, the hard way, that some poems don't rhyme, and some stories don't have a clear beginning, middle, and end. Life is about not knowing, having to change, taking the moment and making the best of it, without knowing what's going to happen next. Delicious ambiguity."
—Gilda Radner

For the first time in my life I had failed at something. I failed at marriage. I couldn't make it work no matter how hard I tried.

I *was* a failure.

Up till that point, life had come fairly easy to me. I was a good kid with a great family. I made practically straight As in high school without a great deal of effort. I was naturally athletic and could pick up almost any sport at will. I was well liked and well received by my peers. I made every team I ever tried out for, got every job I ever wanted. I didn't understand life in anyone else's shoes or life any other way than the way it was *supposed* to go.

I had even looked down on those whose lives didn't come so easily for them. I told myself it was likely their bad choices that led to their circumstances. Or, if their circumstances were truly beyond their control, they were victimizing themselves and needed to grow up.

After my divorce, all the judgement and condemnation I had harbored for others screamed at me from the recesses of my memory. I had been such a hypocrite.

My heart swelled with so much empathy and compassion for my friends and family who had gone through divorces and I wanted to cry for all of us. And still do. I could no longer judge

those who had fallen into adulterous affairs, but now felt
compassionate grace for them as well. I had learned firsthand
how easy it was to look to someone—anyone—for comfort and
affirmation when you were *that* hurt and that lonely in your
own house.

I was humbled.

Worst of all, the dreams I had that I felt God was calling me to
seemed out of reach now. I felt like I was tainted and could no
longer be used by Him at all, at least not for any sort of ministry.
Who would listen to me now? What credibility would I have?
Who could I lead? I couldn't even keep a marriage together!

The First Dream

I was nineteen when I
got the phone call that
my cousin, the one I
looked up to as the
"do-gooder" standard,
was pregnant. Out of
wedlock.

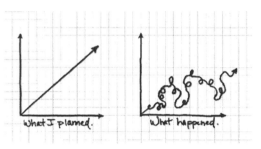

You have to understand that in the religious environment I
grew up in, this was not even close to acceptable. I remember
another church member getting pregnant before her wedding
and wanting to get married at our church. The board members
met and held a vote and told the family no. This was the church
she had spent every Sunday in since her birth. I remember
hearing the talk about her and others in similar situations
behind closed doors. The shame and embarrassment of it. The
audacity they had for even asking! If you had been previously
married, don't even *think* about getting remarried in our church!
Or getting remarried again at all. In fact, you should probably
just quietly disappear because you make the rest of us
uncomfortable with your flagrant sinfulness, as if we were going
to catch it by sitting in the same pew with you. It felt like a

community of Pharisees in a lot of ways.

Have you ever encountered "church people" like this? Have you ever been one?

Even when you're on the inside of that circle, you live with the constant fear and shame of other people finding out about the mess in your life (because we *all* have mess) and wonder what's being said behind the Sunday school doors about you.

Thankfully, that church and the people in it have come a long way spiritually, and to some degree have changed their church policies to reflect a more Christ-like attitude of compassion toward these less-than-perfect members.

But at the time, when I got that call about my cousin, I thought, *If she can't make it to marriage without having sex, what chance do I have?* And then I heard it, as clear as my own voice in my spirit: *No, I will be the example for my younger cousins and nieces. I will show them it is possible. I will never give anyone else a reason to say that about me and make the wrong decision.* I decided to be the standard-bearer for my family.

On that day, a spark was lit in me to speak and teach and train young girls about abstinence in a whole new way than how I was taught at church and at church camp, or the way the public schools teach. *Worth the Wait* was going to be the title of my curriculum with a focus on "Not Mine to Give." (Since your body is the temple of the Holy Spirit, it's not really yours to do with what you please, therefore, your body is not yours to give away to anyone other than your spouse on your wedding night.)

At the time, I didn't even fully understand *why* I was saving my own self for marriage, just that I was "supposed to" and "because the Bible said so," and since I had made the decision not to have sex before marriage and I'm so stubborn, I wasn't going to let *anyone* talk me out of it!

I dreamed of teaching other girls how to assume that responsibility, to make a decision and stand by it, and to understand the personal satisfaction that comes with that resolve.

After my divorce, that dream was crushed. I had followed those rules and stuck by that idea and it didn't work for me, so who the hell would want to follow that plan? I didn't even buy into it anymore.

"So . . . now what, Lord? Now what am I supposed to do with my life?"

Rock Bottom

At the lowest point of my "Now What?" moment, I started doubting the very existence of a god at all. And the thought of that scared the hell out of me. I don't know what was more shocking: the thought that everything I had ever believed in in my life could be a farce or the fact I was so broken I could even ask a question like that, to entertain that idea as a reality. Both terrified me.

In the months after my husband left, I was extremely raw. I was hurt and angry and bitter at God and all His rules. I was mad that I had done everything "His way" and still got screwed over. Things still didn't work out; I still got hurt. I was finished playing by the rules. Have you ever reached this point?

That's when I read a book called *The Shack* by William P. Young. The only way I can describe it is that it was like reading a love letter from God to me.

Without spoiling the story, I will set the scene for you: The main character is a man named Mack, whose past is overshadowed by the pain of a difficult relationship with his father. Mack's young daughter is abducted and murdered by a serial killer, and her blood-stained dress is later found at an abandoned shack in the mountains. He becomes angry and bitter at God. Sometime later he receives a letter, apparently from God, inviting him to come to the shack. Mack makes the journey for a "retreat" to this shack, where he meets the three persons of the Trinity. The bulk of the story is about this encounter and the life lessons Papa God teaches Mack to help him heal.

Be forewarned: In this story, God is a plump, sassy black woman with an affinity for cooking and Eurasian funk music. If that makes the religious hairs on the back of your neck stand up, that's all the more reason you should probably read it.

While reading, it was as if I could hear Papa God saying to me, *No, honey,* this *is who I really am. Everything you think you know about who I am and what I'm like isn't right. That guilt and condemnation, those rules and regulations, that's not Me. Come and get to know Me for yourself.*

And so I did. I was able to start over as a spiritual blank slate and relearned God in a way I had never known Him.

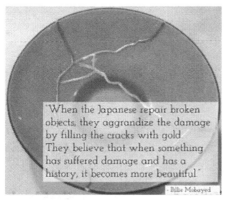

"When the Japanese repair broken objects, they aggrandize the damage by filling the cracks with gold. They believe that when something has suffered damage and has a history, it becomes more beautiful."
— Billie Mobayed

I was overwhelmed by the fact that in all my anger and disgust with God, He still pursued me. He chased after me passionately, relentlessly. *So that's what grace means,* I marveled to myself.

It felt like the greatest romance I had ever experienced. It wasn't until I reached this point in my life where I felt I no longer deserved God's grace that I truly learned to appreciate it. I experienced true freedom for the first time in my life. And then I took *full* advantage of it. Kind of like the way you take full advantage of an all-you-can-eat buffet and then end up with a bellyache later.

Walking in Grace

Once I discovered what grace meant (that was never anything they covered at the church I grew up in), I took a deep dive into a whole new end of the Spiritual Walk pool and began to experience my faith in a way I never had before.

I had a revelation about 1 Corinthians 10:23: "Everything is permissible—but not everything is beneficial. Everything is permissible—but not everything is constructive," and it set me free. I took "everything is permissible" to heart and to an extreme. I decided I could have all the extramarital sex I wanted because, okay, maybe it wasn't such a good idea and I might end up getting hurt, but Jesus still loved me and He wasn't mad at me for it. I didn't have to feel guilty. I figured I had already tried it the "rules and regulations way" and that didn't work out, so what the hell? I was just going to do whatever I want and "walk in grace."

It really was liberating for a while, living with abandon and knowing there was nothing I could do to make God stop loving me, to make Him stop pursuing me. There was no spiritual spanking or cold-shoulder coming because I missed the mark. I finally understood the full meaning of the word *unconditional*.

"I don't know a perfect person. I only know flawed people who are still woth loving."

- John Green

For the first time in my life, I learned how to extend grace to other people. I now understood people I previously would have shunned or condemned and had more empathy for their behavior and actions. Who was I to judge what they were feeling or experiencing? Who was I to say God wasn't okay with it?

During this period, my current husband and I moved in together. We had been dating about a year and a half at that point. I felt no guilt or remorse about it whatsoever. To anyone who was judging me for "living in sin," I wasn't even mad at them; I only felt sorry for them. I thought they were stuck in that condemning religious place that I had been in. They didn't get this "grace thing" yet.

It's funny to joke about now because swimming laps in the

full-on grace pool doesn't really work either. I started to feel something else was missing. No matter how much physical gratification I had, the need for a *deeper* intimacy grew larger and stronger; everything else felt counterfeit and ceased to be enjoyable.

The Believer's Freedom

What Paul is saying in that verse in 1 Corinthians is you can do anything you want, but not everything is going to make you happy, or satisfied, or peaceful, or prosperous.

At that point in my life, I needed to know I wasn't being told "what not to do," that I could make my own decisions and God would still love me and forgive me. What I didn't need was more rules and religion, or guilt and condemnation, but love, grace, and freedom. And in that verse I found it.

There would still be consequences for my actions, which for me was utter unfulfillment. Eventually I realized I was a lot happier doing the things that would bring me closer to God, that would make me more like Him. When I was in tune with Him, I felt more fulfilled and satisfied, which made me want more.

And so there it is, right under the most appropriate heading found in the Bible: "The Believer's Freedom," which is the balance of grace and truth.

In his second work, *Free Book*, Pastor Brian Tome explained how the apostle John said Jesus came to earth "full of grace and truth." Tome went on to describe this symmetry in detail:

> What's so strange about this statement is that the words grace and truth are rarely put together when describing someone. They seem to be a contradiction. Yet they lead to freedom.

> Those known as Grace People cut others a lot of slack. They're the ones you want to be around when you've cheated on your wife or need justification for acting out of

anger. On the other hand, Truth People put others on a tight leash. They're the ones you want around when you're confused and need solid, concrete direction.

Tome listed a table of comparisons, including: "Grace people major in compassion and tend to see the good in everyone. Truth people major in passion and tend to see the good in obedience."

He concluded with:

> We need all that grace has to offer and all that truth has to offer. Yet, experienced separately grace and truth won't offer freedom and will eventually oppress both the giver and the recipient. . . . Taken fully together, grace and truth keep us on the road to wholeness; they're the guardrails that keep us from wrecking our lives with either legalism or antinomianism.[3]

In case you're like me and have no idea what antinomianism means, I went ahead and Googled it for both of us: "In Christianity, an antinomian is one who denies the fixed meaning and applicability of moral law and believes that salvation is attained solely through faith and divine grace. Many antinomians, however, believe that Christians will obey moral law despite being free from it." [4]

YES! (Not that I'm going full-on Antinomianism-an.) But I love that last line, because that's exactly what I learned. Once I was free from all the guilt and condemnation of laws I could never live up to anyway, I was so grateful for grace that I fell more in love with God than I had ever been and wanted nothing more than to please Him.

In the end, I was a "better" Christian without all the expect-ations and pressure of what a "good Christian" is supposed to be.

The Aftermath of Divorce

Since going through my own "D-Day," as I call it, God has put many people in my path who are going through similar situations. They are experiencing a desolate season in their marriage and are considering giving up or leaving, or their spouse has already left. Sometimes they come to me; sometimes I see the telltale signs and reach out to them. Either way, I tell every one of them the same thing: "No matter *how* bad your marriage is, divorce is worse."

The grass isn't greener *on the other side* it's green where you *water & fertilize it.*

- Lysa Terkeurst

As bad as my first marriage was on its worst day—when I felt neglected and lonelier than I ever thought about feeling when I was single, when we had screaming matches every day and literally got into physical altercations, when all I could think about was getting out—divorce was *still* worse.

Even though it seemed like the easiest fix in the short-term—just get out, start over, move on—I never contemplated the long-term aftermath of divorce.

They say love is a battlefield, well divorce certainly is. Divorce takes *every* part of your life backward. You end up in the negative emotionally, financially, relationally, and spiritually. With gaping mortal holes and mounds of debris in each of those areas of your life. You have so much rebuilding to do just to get back to ground zero, much less to move anywhere beyond that. Most people just cover up the craters, or try to stuff other things in them to fill them up, never leveling or solidifying their foundation again. Have you ever tried building anything on an un-even or unstable foundation? How well does that work?

Divorce is truly not worth the havoc that is wreaked in every aspect of your life. When you go through a divorce, every dream you ever had shatters in an instant. You have to start over. Completely. You pick up the broken pieces of your life and your heart and try to figure out how to put them back together in some semblance of order. The only problem is, you have no idea what that looks like now. No idea what "the future" should look like, because the picture you held in your mind for your whole life no longer exists as an option.

The one word that kept coming to my mind the most didn't seem right to me, but it was the only way I could express what I was feeling: *failure*. I felt like a failure. And because I felt like a complete and utter failure, I questioned if I could make anything else in my life work again. I questioned what kind of person I really was.

I thought I was alone in this reaction, but I remember being at a party for my friends' daughter when I learned otherwise. Another dear friend and mentor of mine was there as well, and we found ourselves talking. He quietly and sincerely asked me, "How are you doing?"

"The people with the best advice are usually the ones who have been through the most."

- Unknown

"Good. I'm doing really good."

He saw right through my false positive answer and, with the utmost compassion, said to me, "I remember when I went through my divorce. I just remember feeling like a failure."

Immediately, tears welled up in my eyes as I nodded my head over and over. "Yes, that's exactly what I feel. Those are the exact words I would use."

I don't even remember what else he said to me that day, if he said anything else at all, but he didn't need to. It was the first time I had really talked to anyone about anything I was feeling, and it was the first time I felt like I wasn't alone, like someone understood and could relate to this immeasurable feeling of failure.

In their book *Happily Remarried,* David and Lisa Frisbee said this: "As we work with women who have experienced the end of a marriage, one of the most common themes that emerges is a profound sense of personal failure. Remarkably, even when a woman ascribes most of the blame to her ex-husband, she still manages to internalize a strong sense of shame and regret over her own shortcomings. This can be true even in cases where the wife has been abandoned by a straying husband or deserted by an irresponsible one."

They were singing my song. Too bad I didn't read that book until four years after my divorce. Although I was glad to finally have someone explain it to me, I wish I had found that wisdom sooner.

The Frisbees went on to say, "Men seem far less likely to blame themselves for the end of a relationship and are also much less likely to develop a self-image that centers in personal failure. A man can divorce several times in a row without considering himself at fault. [That made me laugh out loud.] Yet within such a man's unexplored conscience and personal identity there may be significant traces of guilt, self-doubt, and remorse."[5]

Worth Fighting For

During the last nine months of my marriage, Alex and I were still living together but leading separate lives. Surprisingly, we functioned very well as roommates. Once the pressure was off to make our marriage work, he became quite amicable and we became good friends again. We laughed and had fun together. Which made it harder. It made me remember the good times in our relationship and why I fell in love with him in the first place. These painful emotions only made me pursue other relationships to fill that hurtful void even more. I told Alex about every date I went on, longing that he would rise up and fight for me, to want to keep me.

And when that didn't happen, I could only weep silently in my bed alone at night, asking myself "Why am I not worth fighting for? Why doesn't he want me anymore?"

Voices at the Bottom

After it was all over, on top of feeling like a failure, I felt tremendous guilt for ruining my marriage. And my mind constantly raced with thoughts like: *Am I even capable of being married? Am I the type of person who can be in a committed relationship or am I too passionate? Do I get bored too easily? Who would even want to be married to me now, I'm damaged goods.*

When we go through dark seasons in our lives, there is a little voice that comes and whispers in our ears, "You are the only person going through this. You are alone. No one else will understand." And so we withdraw from the world and keep our problems to ourselves.

The more people I meet who open up and share their stories with me, the more I realize there is always someone else going through, or that has gone through, exactly what you're going through.

To my daughter:

If I could give you one thing, it would be the ability to see yourself through my eyes; then you'd see how amazing you truly are.

You are never alone.

Thinking that you are is a cleverly designed lie to drive you into shame, isolation, and depression.

Do not listen to that voice.

I was so plagued by these lies during my divorce that I even started disassociating myself from my leadership team because I felt like the bad apple, a negative influence, and that it was better for everyone if I just wasn't around.

I remember sitting in the parking lot of a training session one night, unable to will myself out of my car and go inside. All those voices were screaming in my head. When suddenly, above all the other voices, I heard clear as day, *These thoughts are not Mine. They are not from Me.*

Have you ever thought something so dark you wondered how it even got in your head?

You see, friend, we have an enemy who wants us to be secluded, alone by ourselves, where he can tear us down and apart. He wants to keep us from other faith-filled people who could build us up and encourage us. If he can bog us down with thoughts of fear, insecurity, worthlessness, and shame, to the point we actually believe we are better off alone, then he wins.

"For our struggle is not against flesh and blood, but against the rulers, against the powers, against the world forces of this darkness, against the spiritual forces of wickedness in the heavenly places" (Ephesians 6:12). And where does this battle take place? In our minds. In our thoughts.

Our thoughts determine our belief systems, and our belief systems determine our actions. If we believe we are worthless or unworthy of love, we often become self-fulfilling prophecies and act in accordance to the way we see ourselves in our minds, which only reinforces those negative thoughts we have.

I could write a whole book about the war that's raging for your thoughts and mine, but Joyce Meyer has already done a great job of that in her classic *Battlefield of the Mind.* I highly recommend it.

Lies and Falsehoods

In my car that night, I took out my notebook and wrote *LIES* in big, bold letters at the top of the page and *Falsehoods* across the next. Then I wrote down every thought that was in my head. Four pages later, this is what I was looking at:

Do any of these sound familiar to you?

- You are not worthy of being loved.
- You can't have the type of love you desire.
- You settled and compromised, so now you just have to take what you can get and deal with it.
- You can never be truly happy in a relationship.
- You're not meant to be tied down.
- You can't be faithful.
- You can't trust yourself.
- You're too needy.
- You want everything you can't have.
- You want too much, expect too much.
- Just settle and be thankful you're loved at all.
- You're damaged goods.
- You have too much baggage.
- You're a hypocrite.
- If they really know who/how you really are, they'd leave you.
- You're too much for anyone to handle.
- You're crazy.
- You're too high maintenance.
- You're too loud.
- You're too strong-willed; too dominating to ever have a strong man.
- You're not worth trying for.
- You're not worth changing for.
- You don't bring out the best in guys.
- You're an attention-addict.
- You have to handle everything on your own.
- No one will take care of you.
- You will never be the "right girl."
- Who would want you now?
- You'll never be good enough.
- You're a failure because you couldn't even make your marriage work.

- You take everyone and everything for granted.
- No one will ever be good enough for you.
- You are so judgmental.
- You can never have a good relationship now because of the bad seeds you've sown.
- Your husband will not be faithful.
- God can't trust you with people; you were not a good steward with who He gave you.
- You will never be happy in a relationship.
- You can never tell your future mate or anyone what you've done; they could never forgive you.
- You are a bad influence and a negative seed.
- It's just better for everyone if you're not around.
- You are not ladylike.
- You can't let anyone see you cry.
- You can't let anyone see weakness in you.
- If you're not perfect, they will be disappointed.
- You are too naïve.
- People will always take advantage of you.
- You don't deserve a good guy.
- There are no such guys like you dream of.
- You are just a hopeless romantic.
- Fairy tales don't come true.
- You are too un-domestic to be a good wife.
- You are too complex; multifaceted.
- No one will ever "get" you.

I looked at the list and the heading at the top of the page, and said out loud, "*None* of these things are true. They are lies from the pit of Hell. In the name of Jesus, I will never entertain these thoughts again."

And I didn't. It was as if I dumped them out, transferred them from my mind to the page when I put them down on that paper. They were out for good. Instantly, my thoughts were clear and organized again. I'm not even certain how to put into words what I experienced that night. It was a very freeing exercise. It was more than just journaling; it was like a mental cleansing. Like hitting the restart button on your computer or phone when it starts running sluggish and erratic because it's bogged down with too much active information.

After that, I told myself I would set out to look up and study all the things God says about me and His promises for my life that countered each of those negative thoughts, each of those lies. I procrastinated doing that right away, so I was left in this weird in-between place. My mind was no longer drowning in a sea of depression and negative, but I certainly didn't believe much positive about myself. I couldn't see how I could be used by God ever again. And I didn't believe in happily ever after.

I put that notebook with the list of lies away and didn't look at it again until I found it about three years later. It was chilling to reread. I was amazed some of those thoughts ever even went through my head! It was like reading words scribbled by a complete stranger, they were so foreign to me. Yet I was reminded by my own handwriting that those were actually thoughts I once had. I thank God I had a revelation about those words spinning around in my head and was able to put a stop to them as early as I did.

"You can't keep a bird from flying over your head, but you can keep it from building a nest in your hair." That quote is often attributed to Martin Luther, and it's so true about our thoughts. We can choose the ones we decide to meditate on and reinforce; we can also choose the ones we decide to dismiss and replace those with *the* Truth.

The Truth Is

A lot of my healing came from books I read like *A Jewel in His Crown* by Priscilla Shirer or *Keeping a Princess Heart in a Not-So-Fairytale World* by Nicole Johnson, music I heard, and even little picture quotes I would see online. But it was a slow and gradual process, and I don't want you to have to linger in that in-between place like me. So recently I asked a friend who is very gifted in studying and discerning God's promises in His Word to help me pull out some of these lies and counter them for you now with scripture. We picked the ones we think are most common, likely some of the ones you recognized as having said to yourself:

Lie: You are not worthy of being loved.

The Truth is: "The LORD appeared to us in the past, saying: 'I have loved you with an everlasting love; I have drawn you with unfailing kindness.'" (Jeremiah 31:3)

"The Lord has chosen you as His treasured possession." (Duet 7:6; *My Paraphrase*)

"This is how God showed his love among us: He sent his one and only Son into the world that we might live through him. This is love: not that we loved God, but that he loved us and sent his Son as an atoning sacrifice for our sins." (1 John 4:9–10)

Lie: You can't have the type of love you desire.

The Truth is: "Delight yourself in the LORD, and he will give you the *desires* of your heart." (Psalm 37:4 ESV, emphasis added)

"The LORD is near to all who call on him, to all who call on him in truth. He fulfills the *desires* of those who fear him; he hears their cry and saves them." (Psalm 145:18–19, emphasis added)

Lie: You're damaged goods.

The Truth is: "Therefore, *if anyone is in Christ, he is a new creation. The old has passed away; behold, the new has come.*"

(2 Corinthians 5:17 ESV, emphasis added)

Lie: If they really know who/how you really are, they'd leave you.

The Truth is: "Be strong and courageous. Do not be afraid or terrified because of them, for the LORD your God goes with you; *he will never leave you nor forsake you.*" (Deuteronomy 31:6, emphasis added)

"Before I formed you in the womb I knew you, before you were born I set you apart." (Jeremiah 1:5)

Lie: You can never have a good relationship now because of the bad seeds you've sown.

The Truth is: "See, I am doing a new thing! Now it springs up; do you not perceive it? I am making a way in the wilderness and streams in the wasteland." (Isaiah 43:19)

Lie: You can never tell your future mate or anyone what you've done; they could never forgive you.

The Truth is: "You, Lord, are forgiving and good, abounding in love to all who call to you." (Psalm 86:5)

You *can* find someone who believes: "Be kind to one another, tenderhearted, forgiving one another, as God in Christ forgave you." (Ephesians 4:32 ESV)

Lie: You can't be faithful.

The Truth is: "I can do all things through Christ who strengthens me." (Philippians 4:13 NKJV)

"But the fruit the Holy Spirit produces is love, joy and peace. It is being patient, kind and good. *It is being faithful* and gentle and having control of oneself." (Galatians 5:22–23, emphasis added)

you are strong,
you are beautiful,
you are worth it,
you have a purpose,
and there is a plan with your name
stamped on it.

Lie: No one will take care of you.

The Truth is: "Cast all your anxiety on him because he cares for you." (1 Peter 5:7)

"The Lord is good, a refuge in times of trouble. He cares for those who trust in him" (Nahum 1:7)

"And my God will meet all your needs according to the riches of his glory in Christ Jesus." (Philippians 4:19)

Lie: You have to handle everything on your own:

The Truth is: "Cast your burden on the Lord (releasing the weight of it) and He will sustain you; He will never allow the righteous to be moved (made to slip, fall or fail)." (Psalm 55:22 AMP)

"You make your saving help my shield, and your right hand sustains me; your help has made me great." (Psalm 18:35)

Lie: You can't let anyone see weakness in you.

The Truth is: "He gives strength to the weary and increases the power of the weak." (Isaiah 40:29)

"But He said to me, 'My grace is sufficient for you, for my power is made perfect in weakness.' Therefore I will boast all the more gladly about my weaknesses, so that Christ's power may rest on me." (2 Corinthians 12:9)

Lie: It's better for everyone if you're not around.

The Truth is: "For I know the plans I have for you," declares the LORD, "plans to prosper you and not to harm you, plans to give you hope and a future." (Jeremiah 29:11)

"And let us not giving up meeting together, as some are in the habit of doing, but encouraging one another—and all the more as you see the Day approaching." (Hebrews 10:25)

Lie: You have too much baggage.

The Truth is: "Create in me a pure heart, O God, and renew a steadfast spirit within me." (Psalm 51:10)"

Lie: You can't let anyone see you cry.

The Truth is: "The Lord will fight for you; you only need to be still." (Exodus 14:14)

Lie: You're too crazy/too loud.

The Truth is: "But the fruit the Holy Spirit produces is love, joy and peace. It is being patient, kind and good. It is being faithful and gentle and having control of oneself. There is no law against things of that kind." (Galatians 5:22–23)

"And the peace of God, which transcends all understanding, will guard your hearts and your minds in Christ Jesus. (Philippians 4:7)

Lie: You can never be happy [in a relationship].

The Truth is: "Rejoice in the Lord always. I will say it again: Rejoice!" (Philippians 4:4)

My Princess.....
YOU ARE SAVED BY GRACE

Don't be so hard on yourself, My love. I see your heart filled with frustration. I know you're in a constant battle between your flesh and your spirit. Don't ever give up trying to live out your faith because of your weaknesses. Don't you know that nothing you do in your own strength will last? I give you grace when you've gone the wrong way, and I give you strength right when you need it. I am here waiting to make all your wrongs right and to heal all your hurts. The battles in your mind belong to Me, so don't waste any more time tearing yourself down. I love you no matter what you've done or said. Now give Me a chance to show you who you are when you are surrendered to Me. Let me give you My gift of grace. Remember that you have been covered with My forgiveness since Calvary; now walk in freedom from the past and open My gift of a new start.

Love,

Your King and Your Grace
[Shari Rose Shepherd, His Princess, Love Letters
from Your King]

Sing a New Song

Music was such an important part of my healing process. And I'm not talking about depressing break-up songs or man-bashing, independent-woman songs, although I can't say that Beyoncé's "Irreplaceable" wasn't played on repeat in my car for a few weeks. But it was the songs that helped me figure out how to get past that bitterness and move on emotionally that were the most life-changing.

I remember the day I pulled back into my office after running out for lunch and heard these lyrics on the radio for the first time: "Do you wonder why you have to, feel the things that hurt you, if there's a God who loves you, where is he now?" *Yes, that's exactly what I'm wondering!* It went on, "Maybe there are things you can't see and all those things are happening, to bring a better ending, someday somehow you'll see. Would you dare would you dare to believe? That you still have a reason to sing 'cause the pain that you've been feeling can't compare to the joy that's coming."[6]

It might have been just a coincidence, but I couldn't help but feel like, at this time in my life when I needed them most, Christian music artists were, for the first time, singing *real* songs with *real* lyrics about *real life* stuff. I'm sure there were songs like that before, but I just wasn't in a place to hear them. The songs I was hearing now were full of words that helped me feel like maybe these people understood what I was going through and had asked some of the same questions, and maybe that didn't make me such a "bad Christian" after all.

It was as if every melody that came into my life at that time was a message straight to me, a great conspiracy of hope.

My sister Karolyn recently typed these words as she shared Sara Bareilles's song "Brave" on her Facebook wall: "Sometimes songs are just that, a song. Sometimes they bring back a memory. Sometimes it's just the beat you love. Sometimes the lyrics mean nothing. Sometimes they mean everything." How true.

Because I know how deeply music helped me heal and gave me hope, I have made "Songs of Hope" mixed CDs for people in my life who are going through their own "Now What?" moments. The gifts have been gratefully received and wildly successful in their purpose.

Sweet friend, if you could tell me your story, I would love to make you your own mixed CD with hand-selected words just for your soul. For now, though, since these pages are all I have with you, I have added a playlist at the end of this chapter. All of the tracks are easily accessible on YouTube, or you can readily download them on iTunes or Amazon Music. No matter how you get them to your ears, do it as quickly as possible, and I assure you, brighter days are just stanzas and song notes away.

In exactly the same way we need to control the thoughts that are already in our heads, controlling the words we let *into* our minds is just as important. For it is the words we let *in* that influence and dictate our thoughts and emotions in the first place. Make sure you are always letting in more positive than negative.

You Are Not Alone

The people who reach out to me sometimes ask me for book recommendations to help them get through this nuclear fallout season of their lives. I tell them the same thing I'm about to tell you. The single most impactful book I read  during that time was *Live, Laugh and Love Again: A Christian Woman's Survival Guide to Divorce*. I only wish there was a male counterpart, but to be honest, I think a guy would get plenty out of *Live, Laugh, and Love Again* too. I know I read tons of highlights to my boyfriend, now husband, as I was making my way through it.

Browsing Amazon for some ray of hope, the title alone begged me to read it. I didn't want to fall into the "bitter, man-hating, divorced-chick" camp of the carnal world, but I didn't really have anywhere to turn. In my life and family, talking about anything as taboo as divorce with another Christian was completely off-limits. The four women who wrote that book became my support group.

I laughed and I cried as I read their stories, but most of all I realized I wasn't alone. And I wasn't crazy. Everything I was thinking and feeling was completely normal. The book explained the different phases you go through during divorce and what to do from there. There is even some advice on what to do if your spouse has expressed a desire for divorce, even if they've left already, but you're not ready to give up.

Along with music, books were my lifeline during that season, and continue to be. Since there are so many wonderful resources out there and it can be overwhelming at times to know what to begin to read, I have also listed the books I found

most helpful in that season at the end of each of the remaining
chapters in this book.

Stay and Fight

"Stay and fight." This has become the final point I've learned that
I tell hurting people who come to me and I want to share with
you. It's absolutely okay to fight for your marriage. You can
always stay a little longer and fight a little harder. What you
don't want is to look back on your life with regret and wish you
had hung in there and given it everything you had.

It's likely that your other
friends are going to tell you
"you deserve better' or that
"you are justified in leaving."
I'm not going to say those
things to you, no matter how
true they may be. I'm going to
tell you it's okay to fight *for*
your spouse. Even if it's not
fair; or they are the one in the
wrong.

Sometimes God
redeems you story by
surrounding you with
people who need to
hear your past, so it
doesn't become their
future.

Jon Acuff

I am giving you permission to stay and fight.

In her book *Girls with Swords*, Lisa Bevere said, "Divorce is
rampant as a generation has decided it is ok to cheat or leave if a
couple feels they are no longer in love. There are attacks on
marriages and within marriages. I can't tell you how many times
John and I have been shocked to hear of couples who apparently
never fought in their marriages but are on the verge of divorce.
We've learned that sometimes a lack of conflict *in* a marriage
means you are not fighting *for* it. There are times you must
battle to become one."[7]

The sad reality is that we are willing to give the best of
ourselves to everyone else in the world, but often neglect the
people in our own home.

As nasty as I was to Alex, there was nothing I wanted more than for him to keep fighting for me. Throughout our whole marriage, there were times one of us would give up, but the other would fight back. The day my marriage ended was not the day Alex left; it was the day we both stopped fighting for each other at the same time.

Stay. Fight. It could literally save you from the nasty fallout of divorce.

"Now WHAT?"

Moment Playlist

With dozens of artists and genres on this list, you're bound to find a style you like, but more importantly, give every song at least one listen and really pay attention to the lyrics. If you don't like the music but the song speaks to you, write down the lyrics in a journal or somewhere where you can see them regularly.

- "Before the Morning," Josh Wilson
- "Safe," Phil Wickham
- "Stronger," Mandisa
- "He Is with You," Mandisa
- "Forgiven and Loved," Jason Needham
- "Beautiful, Beautiful," Francesca Battistelli
- "Hold My Heart," Tenth Avenue North
- "I Need You to Love Me," Barlow Girl
- "Firework," Katy Perry
- "Wanted," Dara Maclean
- "Hero," Mariah Carey
- "You Are More," Tenth Avenue North
- "Hope Now," Addison Road
- "How He Loves," David Crowder Band
- "I Need a Miracle," Third Day
- "I Need You Now," Plumb
- "Yours Forever," Dara Maclean
- "Remind Me Who I Am," Jason Gray
- "Just Cry," Mandisa
- "Let the Waters Rise," Mikeschair
- "The Hurt and the Healer," MercyMe

- "Mirror," Barlow Girl
- "Never Alone," Barlow Girl
- "Not for a Moment," Meredith Andrews
- "Only the World," Mandisa
- "Call My Name," Third Day
- "All This Time," Brit Nicole
- "Gold," Brit Nicole
- "You Carried Me," Building429
- "By Your Side," Tenth Avenue North
- "More Beautiful You," Jason Diaz
- "Hold Me," Jamie Grace
- "Come to Me," Jamie Grace
- "Does Anybody Hear Her?" Casting Crowns
- "Redeemed," Big Daddy Weave
- "Praise You in This Storm," Casting Crowns
- "Blessing in the Storm," Kirk Franklin
- "Born Again," Third Day
- "Busted Heart," For King & Country
- "Forgiven," Sanctus Real
- "Free," Dara Maclean
- "Free to Be Me," Francesca Battistelli
- "By the Grace of God," Katy Perry
- "Healing Begins," Tenth Avenue North
- "Hold Fast," Mercy Me
- "Cry Out to Jesus," Third Day
- "Forgiveness," Matthew West
- "Overcomer," Mandisa
- "Stand in the Rain," Superchick
- "Every Man," Casting Crowns
- "The Climb," Miley Cyrus
- "The Lost Get Found," Brit Nicole
- "While I'm Waiting," John Waller
- "With You," Jamie Grace
- "You Never Let Go," Matt Redman

- "Through the Rain," Mariah Carey
- "How Can It Be," Lauren Daigle
- "Carry You to Jesus," Steven Curtis Chapman
- "Greater," Mercy Me

Recommended Books for

Chapter Four

Books were my own personal therapists that guided me through this journey. I could not get enough of them. I would read through one book and circle all the other book titles they quoted or recommended throughout that spoke to me. Then I ordered and read those. Because I found this so helpful, I will be including a list at the end of each chapter of the books most important to that phase of my journey.

- *Live, Laugh & Love Again: A Christian Woman's Survival Guide to Divorce* by Carla Sue Nelson, Connie Wetzell, Michelle Borquez, and Rosalind Spinks-Seay.
- *The Shack* by William P Young
- *Free Book* by Brian Tome
  Make sure you pick up the accompanying "Free Guide" workbook. We did this as a small group study at my church a few years ago and it absolutely changed my life.
- *Happily Remarried* by David and Lisa Frisbie
- *Battlefield of the Mind* by Joyce Meyer
- *Crash the Chatterbox* by Steven Furtick
- *Girls with Swords* by Lisa Bevere

Resilience Defined

Someone once told me I was the most resilient person they'd ever met. After my divorce, I set out to study that word and embrace it. I couldn't find any definition that encompassed the full value of the word to me, so I wrote my own:

Resilience – /rəˈzilyəns/

Noun: The ability to bounce back, return, or rebound after deterrence or defeat. Buoyancy.
To push through, unscathed and unslighted, any circumstance or situation.
To proceed with resolute determination, giving no regard to attempted diversions, setbacks, letdowns, heartbreaks, poor judgements, unkept promises, or disappointments.
To recover quickly from illness, change, or misfortune.
The ability to spring back after initial plans or anticipations fall through.
To remain standing upright in the smoke-clearing of the battlefield.

The Day I Was the Sun
(Metaphorically Speaking)

The mid-afternoon sky was cluttered with ripples of brush-stroked clouds that day,

But the sky was still light.

Splashes of bright blue broke up the cream and grey colored bodies of dirty air.

The relentless sun made her best effort to escape the shadows.

Beams of luminescence escaped small pockets in the puffy clouds that crowded the yellow ball.

She danced along the outside of their darkening hues—making them three dimensional against their fixed backdrop.

Bright white glowed along the edges of each one,

Hindering their intimidating discoloration.

In all their might,

The clouds tried keeping her hidden that day,

But she was far too tenacious to be averted.

The air was chilled.

Crisp.

As it usually was that time of the year

In the city.

The short-lived days of eighty degrees and sun-filled expanses had passed on,

Giving way to the cooler days of the impending season change.

There was no rain,

Although the clouds looked anxious to deliver.

Despite all the opposing elements,

There she was—

Spilling out beyond the clouds;

So that every eye could see her still

Among the grays that faced the earth's surface.

She saw the brightness

On the back side of the clouds

That others could not yet see.

And the sun, she shined on.

Chapter Five

"Some of the best days of your life
haven't happened yet."

The Redemption

"When plan A fails, God is so amazing that He can make plan B better than plan A ever could have been!"
–Joyce Meyer

It was another warm day in May. I was working from my home office. My boyfriend, Barry, came home from work and asked what I'd like to do that night. When I said, "I don't know," he suggested we go on a walk.

"Okay," I said, still working on my laptop.

"Hurry up! I want to go on a walk *right now!*"

Sometimes Barry gets, well, *squirrely*, I call it. When he can't sit still and needs to be doing *something*. So I just assumed this was one of those times. I got up from my desk and went to my closet to change clothes. I put on a pair of my comfortable ripped jeans and a tank top.

"Maybe you'd like to wear a sundress," he said.

"To walk around the neighborhood?"

I walked into the bedroom to find him putting on a button-up dress shirt with his jeans. "What are you wearing?" I asked. "You're going to be so hot in that! What is wrong with you right now?"

He changed. We walked.

We talked about his day at work and mine, our travel plans for the weekend.

As we came around the corner to our house, he suggested we go in the backyard to lay in our hammock and talk. This was not an uncommon thing for us to do. After a few minutes, he got up and said, "Stay right there. I have a surprise for you!" Also not uncommon.

He returned with something he had hidden behind our fire pit. I unwrapped the box to find a hand-made leather journal with my initials branded in the front. My *future* initials. I thought, *Well, we're going to be married* some*day, so that's smart.* He also gave me a really nice refillable fountain pen with my favorite animal, a giraffe, print on it. I laughed and said, "This is to replace the fountain pen of mine you lost!"

I flipped to the front page of the journal to find a note explaining that the purpose of the journal was for me to document our continued travel adventures together with pictures and words. Then I flipped to the second page and saw he had written, "Will you marry me?"

As I looked up from the page, I saw him getting down on one knee and pulling a gorgeous ring from his pocket. He said some other sweet things and slipped the ring on my finger. I said yes. We kissed and took pictures in the hammock. And then we heard, "Welllll, ain't that a Kodak moment!" from the top of the hill by our neighbor Brad.

God Loves to Bring Things Full Circle

But this isn't the end of the story yet either. Contrary to what you might have imagined, this is not the happily ever after I referred to in the introduction. Keep reading, dear one. We're just getting started.

Recommended Books for
Chapter Five

- *Beauty for Ashes* by Joyce Meyer
- *Keeping a Princess Heart in a Not-So-Fairytale World* by Nicole Johnson
  It was so important to me not to let my heart and spirit become bitter during my divorce, and this book really helped me learn how to do that.
- *A Jewel in His Crown* by Priscilla Shirer
- *Make Your Dreams Bigger Than Your Memories* by Terri Savelle Foy
  I literally laughed out loud at God's sense of humor when I saw the title of this book for the first time.
- *Joy That Lasts* by Gary Smalley
- *Choose Joy Because Happiness Isn't Enough* by Kay Warren

Chapter Six

"You can't start the next chapter of your life if you keep re-reading the last one."

- Unknown

The Freak-out
I'm Not Ready for This!

I wish I could tell you when Barry got on his knee and asked me to marry him that I cried, that I was overwhelmed with joy and excitement.

That's not what happened.

In that Kodak moment, dozens of emotions flooded through my mind and heart, none of them fitting for the occasion. Sheer panic and terror: those were the first things that raced through my synapses. Next, heaps of guilt and anxiety weighed down on my shoulders. Then, worst of all, I felt guilty for not reacting the *right* way and ruining what should have been one of the happiest moments of his life!

My reaction should not have shocked me, though. For months leading up to that day, my thoughts had already been scrambled about our relationship. His question only pushed my uncertainty into overdrive. I couldn't stop the mental ping-pong in my head.

Early in our relationship, while contemplating whether it was the right time to get serious, as I was fresh out of my marriage, Barry asked me, "How do I know we won't get six months down the road and you'll decide you should have taken a break after your divorce and you'll dump me?" I unrealistically promised him, "That won't happen." Now my own words haunted me.

What if I *did* need to be single for a while to clear my head and figure things out?

Our relationship was wonderful by most standards. We

hardly ever fought, and if we did it was short-lived and never escalated to an unhealthy level. He was always quick to resolve a disagreement and make peace. We *should* have been happy.

But every time I was alone with my thoughts, I wondered if there was someone "better" out there. Although I was terrified of finding out that person didn't exist.

WAITING FOR SOMEONE ELSE TO *make you happy* IS THE BEST WAY TO BE SAD
-unknown

I just kept playing out in my mind what would happen if I told him I needed to take a break or date around. I knew that would absolutely crush him. Then, by the time I was ready to be in a serious relationship again, he surely would have found and fallen in love with someone else and I would regret letting such a good guy go.

Chick-flick and Stephanie Meyer novel scenes played on repeat in my mind, revealing that our relationship was painfully lacking the sizzle and romance I knew we *should* have, according to those standards. Wasn't *that* what relationships are supposed to look like, to feel like?

I had even reached a point where I was unable, and honestly unwilling, to pray about our relationship. Anytime I would pray about any other part of my life, I would be bombarded with the thoughts, *I need to pray about Barry, about us. I need some peace and clarity.* But I'd talk myself out of it. I was certain God was going to tell me to break up with him. So I decided if I didn't pray about our relationship at all, I wouldn't have to hear that answer, and then I wouldn't be living in disobedience. If you're laughing right now, I'm sure it's because you've done this before too, and you already know it doesn't work like that.

I thought maybe the reason I had lost my interest in and physical desire for Barry was because God was trying to get me to leave him and end our relationship. It's not like I could ask God to give me passionate longings for my boyfriend with whom

I was living *out of wedlock*! Eventually I just didn't pray at all so I wouldn't feel the guilt of not praying for the thing I knew I really needed to be praying for. Sound familiar?

> *You can't do anything so bad it will cause God to love you any less.*
>
> *- Dr. James Merritt*

The whole thing had become so mentally incapacitating that I initiated the idea we stop having sex. I thought our physical relationship was clouding my ability to make a clear judgement, fogging my mind with romanticism that didn't actually exist. I reasoned that if we cut off sex, I would be able to think clearly and figure out what I actually felt about him and where we were going. Since our relationship had started so physically, I needed to know we actually had something of substance beneath all of that. Barry was surprisingly onboard with the idea.

We were about six months into this no-sex experiment when he proposed. But my mind was no clearer. Nor had our relationship ignited any magical flames of intimacy. We still did day-to-day life together and slept in the same bed, just with our clothes on now. Things had not gotten better—or worse, for that matter. They were just ... blah.

Brian Tome has this insight into part of what we may have been experiencing at the time in *Free Book*:

> Usually we have sex because, in the moment, we feel like it'll be a freeing experience. So we agree to trade our bodies. But ultimately if we're not in a marriage, it only results in memories and emotional carnage that we'll have to spend a long time healing from. It will be something we'll want to hide from the person we truly love in a few years—and that produces guilt and shame. It's the same for affairs. Often people jump at having an affair because it seems to promise intense excitement. But there is immediate fallout to deal with once it's over, and

it becomes clear that it was just a form of false freedom. [*Can I get an amen!*] I'm not just talking about "unwanted pregnancies"—I'm talking about the emotional baggage such as rejection, loneliness, worthlessness, anger and jealousy to name a few.

All change, in the moment, can look like failure. So when you choose to stop having sex with someone to whom you're not married, some feelings of abandonment, coupled with dissatisfaction and confusion will probably settle in. But you have to go through those emotions because that's what freedom usually looks like in the first stages. It looks like it will be worse than what you had before. So you have to hang in there for the blessings, because they, too, will come.[8]

Man, did I go through every phase of that emotional rollercoaster he was describing! I certainly hadn't made it to the blessing stage yet when Barry gave me that ring.

We were in a rut. And I was once again disillusioned with lasting relationships.

This Ain't Disneyland

Since my divorce, I had come to grips with the fact that life is not a fairy tale. I had refused to let bitterness harden my heart, but I was completely and utterly disenchanted with the whole idea of marriage. I didn't believe in happily ever after anymore. I didn't believe in "soul mates" or God saving one special person for you your whole life.

Life is not a fairy tale.

If you lose your shoe at midnight, you're drunk.

Tome humorously addressed this as well:

When I was in college, I lived with a bunch of Christ-following guys who were training for ministry. One of the stupider things I did during that time of my life was mindlessly fall into the assumption that I should be doing what the other guys were doing. They were all getting married young, so I assumed I should get married young. This meant that every girl I ran across who was halfway decent looking and claimed to follow Jesus was likely the one. At this point in my life, I believed that God had one perfect mate picked out for everyone. Some people call this a "soul mate," I now call this a "bad idea."

I can't even describe how hard I laughed the first time I read that last sentence. Tome went on:

If you get married and believe that person is the only person God would have been happy about you marrying, your opinion is likely to change about one year into the relationship when you realize there are thousands of other people who would have been just as capable. In my wife Libby's case, there were hundreds of thousands of other guys more capable than I.[8]

I had experienced exactly what he was talking about. At this point, I had also begrudgingly accepted the fact that when you marry someone, the infatuation you first felt when you started dating wanes and steadies out into more of a friendship, a partnership.

So I get it. The "butterflies" don't last forever. I can handle that. I admitted to myself that I had run from relationship to relationship my whole life chasing those butterflies, and as soon as they were gone, I'd drop that guy and move on to the next. Because of that, I had made the decision to stick it out with Barry no matter how I felt. More than anything else to prove to myself I could, to trust myself again. But was that any reason to stay with someone, out of obligation? Or some test of character?

When I really thought about all of this, I would feel bitter and cheated; I wanted to feel that romance, that passion, even if I knew it wasn't reality. Was I settling? And if so, was that fair to Barry? If I wasn't really in love with him, should I let him move on and be with someone who would be? Had I ever been in love with Barry? Did that even matter?

Around and around this mental merry-go-round went. Knowing that "real" relationships weren't based on feelings, but longing for them anyway; deciding to stay regardless of my lack of romantic feelings, although begrudgingly.

I'm Engaged, Now What?

I accepted Barry's proposal, but I couldn't stop reeling at the thought that maybe I hadn't made the right decision. Not only was I unsure about him, I was even more unsure about marriage. Did I even want to be married again? Could I be married again? What was the point? What did marriage even mean? I'd already tried marriage once and it sucked. Bad. I thought I'd married "the one" and it still didn't work out.

I also reasoned Barry and I were perfectly content the way we were. Why did we have to get married and ruin it? I knew as long as we weren't married, if he ever changed and became a completely different person (like my first husband had), I could just walk away. But if we were married, I was stuck, no matter how terrible it became. Because I sure as hell wasn't going to be the twice-divorcée.

> BEFORE
> ALICE GOT TO
> WONDERLAND
> SHE HAD TO
> FALL
> PRETTY HARD
> DOWN A
> DEEP HOLE.
> -UNKNOWN

The night we got engaged, while lying in bed *not* sleeping, I got on Amazon.com from my phone and ordered every Christian-looking book I could find on divorce and remarriage. One of them was literally called *I Love You, but I'm Not in Love with You: 7 Steps to Saving Your Relationship*. That one was the only title I was a little concerned about Barry seeing come in the mail.

The next day we headed in separate directions: I went to Chicago for a tradeshow and Barry went to Alabama for a men's retreat.

Where It All Began

A whole two tons of gut-wrenching irony hit me as I started an entry into my new journal from my hotel room in Chicago. As I wrote the date—May 20, 2013—I realized I had met my first husband on that exact date seven years earlier, at that train station downtown, less than two miles from where I was sitting. And here I was, seven years later, married and divorced from that sailor and freshly engaged again. What was I thinking?!

While in town, I had dinner with my friend Charlene and spewed every detail of every thought, positive and negative, I had had in the last forty-eight hours, really the last several months.

I told her I was thinking of going to a Christian divorce therapist since I never went to one immediately following my divorce. She affirmed that was definitely a good idea; she had done the same after her divorce years prior and it had been a big help. For that night, though, Charlene *was* my therapist. She listened patiently, as only a truly great friend can.

She advised I needed to have a talk with Barry and stop hiding what I had been feeling. Although she did caution that there were certain thoughts and feelings I should reserve from telling him (like that I wasn't certain if I had *ever* been in love with him). She also recommended we start doing weekly date nights to build up the intimacy and communication that was lacking in our relationship.

> "More people would learn from their mistakes if they weren't so busy denying them."
>
> -Harold J. Smith

Just like writing out all the lies I had been telling myself during my divorce helped me gain clarity on what I was thinking and feeling and see the truth, being able to get all my concerns, doubts, and uncertainties out of my head and into words with Charlene helped me process everything into more concise thoughts.

Thinking Clearly

Here are the things I did know:

I loved Barry with all my heart and wanted to spend the rest of my life with him.

I had done an exceptionally poor job at really dealing with the fallout of my divorce. I had just ignored it, kept moving forward, sprinted away from the carnage. I worked to reassemble my life to some reflection of normality as soon as possible and hadn't taken the time to stop and think about the ramifications of it all.

The one thing I absolutely knew for sure was that I wanted and *needed* to get all the emotional residue from my first marriage sorted out before I walked down the aisle again. I refused to carry any emotional baggage into my marriage with Barry.

I admitted I didn't understand the purpose or point of marriage, and I needed to study what God's design for that really was.

And finally, I decided once and for all that there really are no such things as fairy tales. I had already experienced that firsthand. No relationship was going to be rainbows and butterflies all the time. I was going to have to *work* to keep the spark alive, no matter *who* I was with.

I concluded I wanted to be with Barry. I wanted him to be the one with whom I would *make* it work. I wanted to fall in love with him.

All this was easier said than done. I didn't even know where to start!

The Talk

When I came home from Chicago, I sat Barry down to have the potentially relationship-ending conversation with him that I had already had with Charlene. I agonized as all the thoughts and

conflicting emotions I had hidden from him came out. I wept as I thought about the damage every word was doing to him as it poured out of my heart, through my mouth, to his ears. I could barely form the syllables through the tears as I stared down at my hands and struggled to explain.

"Barry, our relationship is so backward. We started as friends, and then we started having sex because I was lonely and had a void that needed to be filled from the disintegration of my marriage. Then we kind of started dating, but you were bartending so we couldn't date on weekends like normal people and we just hung out in your apartment. Then we moved in together because it was so convenient. Now it's, like, sure we should get married because that's the next logical step and it's been the acceptable amount of time, but our relationship is so bland, it's just friendship and sex. And I want more than that. I need more than that. I know every relationship has a honeymoon phase that ends, but I don't even know when ours was or if we even had one! We're in a rut, and I need to know we can get out of it, and that we can have that passion I so desperately need. Because right now I'm not so sure. And then you had the unfortunate timing of proposing while we are in this rut!"

I paused. He hadn't walked out the door or thrown anything

so I barged on.

"I just don't feel like we ever had that chance to date for real and fall in love. I feel like we need to slow down. I almost wish we could back up and start over. I wish we could date and then fall in love, and *then* we can talk about getting married!"

I ran out of things to say but kept crying. My heart was broken at the thought of annihilating his. Silence. I peeked my eyes up at him, but didn't dare raise my head. What on earth was going through his mind? I thought for sure I had just ended our relationship and he was going to announce that he would move out.

Instead, he broke his contemplative silence with, "Shhh. Come here, don't cry." He came close to me and pulled me to his chest. "You don't need to cry. We can start over," he said. "I'd like that."

"Really?"

"Yeah, I'd love to date you. We can do that."

I started to wipe my eyes, there was another silent pause, and the next thing I knew, he backed up, straightened, and stuck out his

"We cannot start over, but we can begin now, and make a new ending."
-Zig Ziglar

hand. "Hi. My name's Barry." Shaking my hand, he pointed and said, "That's my dog, Major. It's nice to meet you."

In that moment, I really did fall in love with him.

However, moments are fleeting, and human beings are fickle and selfish and short-tempered. It takes a lot more than one sweet romantic gesture (no matter how heart-throbbing) to keep a marriage together for the long haul. And we cannot do it at all by our own strength and power. That's exactly what I would go on to learn on my journey of preparing for my remarriage over the next six months.

Starting from Scratch

After that conversation, we did start over. We started going on weekly date nights and having real conversations. Not just about our plans for the weekend or our to-do lists for the house. We worked through a book I had ordered called *1001 Questions to Ask Before You Get Married* by Monica Leahy on a lot of these dates, which sparked some very pertinent and meaningful conversations.

I had one stern ultimatum prior to our nuptials. I made Barry a list of five books that he *had* to read before we said "I do." They were books I had been asking him to read since we started dating, which he had procrastinated doing. More than anything, I wanted to know he could follow through on a promise of this kind. That he'd hold himself accountable and see it to completion. Promise keeping was a major source of conflict and struggle in my marriage with Alex, and I knew how debilitating it was to the trust in our relationship. Barry was a reader and expressed interest in reading those books; he just hadn't had any sense of urgency about it up till that point. Once I was able to set a firm deadline, it was time to see if he was really serious and able to keep a commitment.

Besides that, I knew these books would help him understand me a little better, as a woman and a choleric-sanguine personality, and even get a better understanding of himself, therefore preventing a lot of potential conflict.

The five books were *Personality Plus* by Florence Littauer, *The Five Love Languages* by Gary Chapman, *Love & Respect* by Emerson Eggrichs, *His Needs, Her Needs* by Willard Harley, and *Wild at Heart* by John Eldredge. I ended up adding a sixth as I read it and learned how valuable it was to our premarital journey: *Saving Your Marriage Before It Starts* by Les and Leslie Parrott.

Saving Your Second Marriage Before It Starts had been one of the first books I ordered that sleepless night of our engagement. I absolutely could not stop talking about it. I honestly think the Parrotts' material should be required reading for every dating or engaged couple. If only I had known about the things they coach couples to contemplate prior to my first marriage, how much turmoil and heartache could I have been spared! I found their accompanying workbooks for men and women, and Barry and I were able to work through those together on date nights. They were a tremendous blessing.

When we started our premarital "Building Blocks" course at our church, we were so far ahead of the other hundred-plus participants in the class because of those books we had already read and studied together. We were even asked to volunteer teaching in future classes!

Sobering Statistics

The Introduction of the Parrotts' book sets up the dire need for itself and other books of the like:

> In the 1930s, one out of seven marriages ended in divorce. In the 1960s, it was one out of four. Of the 2.4 million couples who will get married this year in the United States, it is predicted that at least 43 percent will not survive. For too many couples, marriage has become "till divorce do us part."

> Every couple marrying today is at risk. More than two-hundred thousand new marriages each year end prior to the couple's second anniversary. After they toss the bouquet and return the tuxedos, couples often assume they're headed for marital bliss. But a study of those who recently tied the knot revealed that 49 percent reported having serious marital problems. Half were already having doubts about whether their marriage would last.

The truth is, most engaged couples prepare more for their wedding than they do for their marriage. The $50-billion-a-year wedding industry can testify to that fact. . . . More than one million copies of bridal magazines are sold each month, focusing mainly on wedding ceremonies, honeymoons, and home furnishings—but not on marriage itself.[9]

What a shame. No wonder we've got generations of couples and families being torn apart by the tragedy of divorce. I was determined to rightly prepare myself as much as humanly possible before I said "I do" again.

Recommended Books for

Chapter Six

- *Saving Your Marriage Before It Starts* (or Saving Your Second Marriage Before It Starts, whichever applies to your situation) by Les and Leslie Parrott
I would definitely recommend getting the accompanying workbooks for men and women.
- *1001 Questions to Ask Before You Get Married* by Monica Leahy
- *Personality Plus* by Florence Littauer
- *The Five Love Languages* by Gary Chapman
- *Love & Respect* by Dr. Emmerson Eggrichs
- *His Needs, Her Needs* by Willard F. Harley, Jr.
- *Wild at Heart* by John Eldredge
Although written specifically for men, it's a very insightful read for a woman.
- *Captivating* by Stasi Eldredge
This is the female counterpart to *Wild at Heart*. It helps you understand why you do the things you do and why you want the things you want. It's not because you are crazy or even "too needy" but because that's exactly the way God created you, on purpose, as a woman.

Chapter Seven

"You turned my wailing into dancing
You removed my sackcloth and clothed me with joy,
that my heart may sing your praises and not be silent.
Lord my God, I will praise You forever.

- Psalm 30:11-12

The Myth of Prince Charming and Other Lies We've Been Told

"'And they lived happily ever after' is one of the most tragic sentences in literature. It's tragic because it's a falsehood. It is a myth that has led generations to expect something from marriage that is not possible."
—Joshua Liebman

Once upon a time, long, long ago, in a bedroom not-so-far away, you were told a bedtime story of a prince who would come for you, sweep you off your feet, and rescue you from your ordinary life and all the wrong guys you would date. You would exchange your vows at the wedding of your dreams and ride off into the sunset on horseback to live happily ever after.

That story was then reiterated through every movie you ever saw, every book you ever read, every magazine article ever published, and even every youth group meeting you ever attended.

The only problem with riding off into the sunset is that after the sun sets and night falls, the next day morning comes. And this person you thought was perfect wakes up with morning breath and bed head, leaves his underwear on the bathroom floor, squeezes your toothpaste tube the wrong way, leaves the toilet seat up,

Some day, you'll meet a man, and he'll sweep you off your feet and promise you the world. You just punch that lying bastard as hard as you can and run, baby!

and then saunters into the kitchen expecting you to produce a hot breakfast.

Months like this go by, and each night he comes home from work, expects you to have cooked again, and then sits down to watch ESPN highlights or surf the Internet rather than planning a romantic date or doing the things he promised you he would get done around the house.

Reality hits and disenchantment sets in as you realize you have to live with this person for the rest of your life.

Does this sound familiar to you?

I had bought the Disney fairy-tale dream hook, line, and sinker. And I had paid dearly for it. I wanted to set Walt Disney's gravestone on fire!

While the scenario I described above may seem more like a nightmare than a fairy tale, and even a bit cynical, it doesn't have to be this way.

Setting Right Expectations

In chapter 1 of *The Power of a Praying Wife*, author Stormie Omartian said, "The biggest problems in my marriage occurred when my expectations of what I thought Michael should be or do didn't coincide with the reality of who he was."[10]

Mary Laner, a professor of sociology at Arizona State University, agreed that we expect too much. Laner said that when the marriage or the partner fails to live up to our ideals, we don't recognize that our expectations were much too high. Instead, we blame our spouse or that particular relationship.

"We think that our partner can meet all our needs, know what we're thinking, and love us even when we're not terribly lovable. When those things don't happen, then we blame our partner," Laner said. "We think that maybe if we had a different spouse, it would be better." Is she reading your thoughts as clearly as she was reading mine?

The sociologist studied the marital expectations of

unmarried college students. She compared their expectations with those of people who have been married for about ten years. The significantly higher expectations held by the students, she said, come straight out of the "happily ever after" fantasy.

"And," she added, "many of us continue to take our zealous ideas of what marriage should be into the next relationship and the next, and so on.

"People who marry again following divorce, one might think, would not carry along inflated expectations," Laner said. "Yet, these second and later marriages have higher divorce rates than do first marriages. As far as expectations are concerned, this may be a reflection of the primacy of hope over experience, followed once again by disillusionment."[11]

Don't get me wrong, it's very normal and natural to have the expectation and desire that the way your spouse was before you got married will stay the same. "When two people get married, each partner has a right to expect the same loving care and attention that prevailed during courtship to continue after the wedding," author Willard F. Harley Jr. stated.

He continued, "Every husband and wife need to sit down and meditate on this thought: My partner married me because she or he thought the pleasing things I was doing during our courtship would continue for the rest of our lives. Am I holding

---

Marriage Box

"Most people get married believing a myth that marriage is a beautifl box full of all the things they have longed for: companionship, intimacy, friendship, etc. The truth is that marriage at the start is an empty box. You must put something in before you can take anything out. There is no love in marriage. There is no romance in marriage. You have to infuse those things into your marriage. A couple must learn the art and form the habit of giving, loving, serving, praising, keeping the box full. If you take out more than you put in, the box will be empty."

- Unknown

up my end of this bargain?

Most people who marry do not assume that their courtship has been a fantasy and that, after marriage, everything will become terrible. They marry because they have enjoyed what happened during the courtship so much that they want it to continue for life."[12]

It is also *not* fair or reasonable, or even wise, to go into your marriage expecting your husband or wife will change into something he or she is not.

I remember reading an article that talked about how important it is to keep your eyes open during dating and to foster right expectations in marriage. It said something like, "The cute little quirks your boyfriend has will suddenly become unacceptable for a husband, and your girlfriend who can't cook is not likely to become Martha Stewart on your wedding day." Even if they tell you that's their desire, you have to be willing to accept them if it never happens.

I tell dating couples that they need to take enough time to get to really know each other. See their partner in lots of different situations, around different people. See their good, their bad, and their ugly. See them angry and disappointed. Be honest about the things you don't like about them and then soberly ask yourself, "If they never change, can I handle this for the rest of my life?" If the answer is no, you need to walk—no, run—away, right now.

I got married the first time thinking my husband and I would grow and change and mature together over the years, so never mind those pesky little habits or character flaws he had. Surely as soon as we were married, he would realize those were things that only bachelors did, and if he didn't, I could point them out and he would step right in line, thankful to have such a great husband-coach under his roof, someone so committed to helping him become a better person.

Turns out that's not even close to what happened. I learned

the jarring reality that you're never changing anyone. Ever. Under any circumstance, whatsoever. And if someone appears to change to suit your expectations, it won't be genuine. It will likely be temporary, and they will develop bitterness and resentment toward you for it.

Stormie Omartian said this of her own experience:

> I thought I had married a man who was close to perfect and what wasn't perfect was cute. As time went on, cute became irritating and perfect became driving perfectionism. I decided that what irritated me most about him had to be changed and then everything would be fine.

> It took a number of years for me to realize my husband was never going to conform to my image. It took a few years beyond that to understand I couldn't make him change in any way. In fact, it wasn't until I started going to God with what bothered me that I began to see any difference at all.

All that you can do is continue to grow and better yourself, which has the potential to inspire the *desire* to grow and change in the other person. But that has to be *their* idea. You can awaken a man's desire to want to be better for you, and that's wonderful. But I think he still needs to have a stronger motive than pleasing you for it stick long-term. And I believe that's where prayer comes in.

Omartian stressed the message of her book, the power of prayer: "It took me a number of years to learn what millions of women have learned over the centuries. Nagging doesn't work! Criticizing doesn't work. Sometimes, just plain talking doesn't accomplish anything either. I've found that prayer is the only thing that always works."[13]

Prayer is what gives you peace before anything changes or while the change is happening, or helps you see that you're the one who needs to make a change. *Ouch*! Because again, the only thing you can control is *your* actions and *your* attitude.

Never enter into a marriage relationship with someone you *need* to change in order to be happy because that's not going to end well for either of you.

"I'm all for forgiveness and grace. And I believe that people change. But I don't believe that people change people. And I don't believe that people change for people. People change themselves. People change themselves when they get sick and tired of themselves, when the pain of staying the same is too great to bear or there's a goal so enticing that it draws them away from what and who they used to be," said Andy Stanley in *The New Rules for Love, Sex and Dating*.[14]

Things I Wish I Knew Before I Got Married

Just recently I ran across an article online titled "10 Things Married People Want Couples to Know Before They Commit" that said, "Lust may ebb & flow but the friendship and gratitude never should," and I found myself cheering and amen-ing as I read. I think it highlights several of the lessons I learned in my premarital study. The author, Vicki Santillano, wrote,

> Even if you've been with someone for a long time, marriage can still seem like a scary endeavor. More than one person will tell you that marriage changes everything, that marriage is "work," and you won't understand what that really means. Can a piece of paper and a couple of rings make that much of a difference? For some couples, absolutely; others, not so much. It's all a matter of expectations and, of course, those delightful curveballs life loves to throw at us.
>
> Whether you're considering a walk down the aisle, otherwise committing to someone for the long haul, or want to know what to look for in your next relationship,

there's important advice you need to know. Who better to dish it out than people who've been there already?

Santillano pulled together tidbits from an old Reddit thread asking, "What's the best piece of advice you could offer to a couple?" The two that most jumped out at me were:

- "Most of the time you spend together is going to be non-sexual, so you better be best friends, or it won't last."

- "You may love her long blonde hair, her perfect smile and her great figure but the body changes over time and life throws curves. If you don't think you can handle the changes that life will bring then you aren't in love, you are in lust."[15]

Can I get an amen? This is great advice!

While I had read many books like this on relationships and marriage prior to my first wedding, I never read any books or received any advice on how to *prepare* myself for marriage. I'm sure I am not alone in this, and it's truly a tragedy.

There's a big difference between understanding concepts of how to communicate, how to resolve conflict, how to meet your spouse's specific needs, etc., versus having right expectations of what marriage truly is and isn't.

"The truth is that the more intimately you know someone, the more clearly you'll see their flaws. That's just the way it is. That's why marriages fail, why children are abandoned, why friendships don't last. You might think you love someone until you see the way they act when they're out of money or under pressure or hungry, for goodness' sake. Love is something different. Love is choosing to serve someone and be with someone in spite of their filthy heart. Love is patient and kind. Love id deliberate. Love is hard. Love is pain and sacrifice. It's seeing the darkness in another person and defying the impulse to jump ship."
- Anonymous

I think the biggest problem facing marriages today, at least in Western culture, is nothing more than inaccurate expectations. If your expectations are realistic and appropriate, then you won't be so disappointed and disenchanted when you hit a diversion or detour in the road to happily ever after.

During my premarital journey, I stumbled upon a book by Gary Chapman called *Things I Wish I'd Known Before We Got Married*, in which he speaks about many of the things I was thinking and experiencing.

The first two things he wished he'd known (and boy, do I wish I had as well!) were (1) being in love is not an adequate foundation for building a successful marriage, and (2) romantic love has two stages.

Chapman wrote:

> Before I got married, no one informed me that there were two stages of romantic love. I knew that I was in love with Karolyn and I anticipated having these feelings toward her for the rest of my life. I knew that she made me happy and I wanted to do the same for her. When in fact I came down off of the emotional high, I was disillusioned. . . . I was plagued with the recurring thought, "I have married the wrong person." I reasoned that if I married the right person, surely my feelings would not have subsided so quickly after marriage. These were painful thoughts that were hard to shake. *Our differences seem so obvious now. Why did I not see them earlier?*

> I wish someone had been there to tell me what I was thinking and feeling was normal; in fact, there are two stages to romantic love and I had to make the transition . . . the second stage of romantic love is much more intentional than the first. And, yes, it requires work in order to keep emotional love alive.[16]

Not Your Typical Love Triangle

Les and Leslie Parrott explain this progression and balance of love in relationships from passion to intimacy to commitment in their book *Saving Your Marriage Before It Starts*.

> Whatever love is, it is not easy to pin down, for love is a strange mixture of opposites. It includes affection and anger, excitement and boredom, stability and change, restriction and freedom. Love's ultimate paradox is two beings becoming one, yet remaining two.

> We have found love's paradoxical quality makes some couples question whether they are really in love. We meet dozens of engaged and married couples in this predicament every year...

> ...A few years ago, it was much more difficult to answer this question. Fortunately, the study of love has become more respectable in recent years and is no longer taboo. Today, hundreds of studies and professional articles on love are being published each year. And there is much to be gleaned from the scientific harvest.

> Robert Sternberg, a Yale University psychologist, has pioneered much of the new research. He developed the triangular model of love, one of the most encompassing views to date. In his model, love, like a triangle, has three sides: passion, intimacy and commitment....

> ...Passion, intimacy, and commitment are the hot, warm, and cold ingredients in love's recipe. And these ingredients vary, because the levels of intimacy, passion, and commitment change from time to time and from person to person.

> You can visualize the fluidity of love by considering how the love triangle changes in size and shape as the 3

components of love increase and decrease. The triangle's area represents the amount of love.

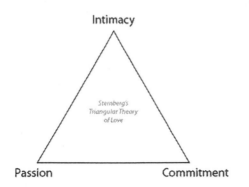

Large amounts of intimacy, passion and commitment yield a large triangle. The larger the triangle, the more the love.

The Parrotts go on in that chapter to explain how a love relationship changes as one side of the triangle shrinks or grows larger at times, and the different "kinds" of love relationship that type of triangle represents. Geometry refresher aside, it's fascinating.[17]

It just goes to show that when people say they are "out of love," it likely just means they are out of sync with the *type* of love they are currently experiencing with their spouse.

In another chapter of *Things I Wish I Knew…*, Chapman gave me hope about the romantic love for which I was still yearning. He said, "Please do not misunderstand me. I think the tingles are important. They are real, and I am in favor of their survival. But they are not the basis for a satisfactory marriage. I am not suggesting that one should marry without the tingles. Those warm, excited feelings, the chill bumps, that sense of acceptance, the excitement of the touch that make up the tingles serve as the cherry on top of the sundae. But you cannot have the sundae with only the cherry."[18]

The Three Marriage Lies

After I began writing this chapter, I received an invitation from Proverbs 31 Ministries to participate in a five-day challenge of "Praying Boldly for Your Marriage." Day 2 floored me, as I was writing about the very topics it covered. Proverbs 31 founder, Lysa TerKeurst, shared her story in the e-mail:

I know the heart-ripping hopelessness of a relationship unraveling. The coexisting. The silent tension. The tears.

The first five years of my marriage were really hard. Two sinners coming together with loads of baggage, unrealistic expectations and extremely strong wills.

There was yelling. There was the silent treatment. There were doors slammed. There was bitterness. There was a contemplation of calling it quits. There was this sinking feeling that things would never, could never get better. That's when I first started hearing the 3 lies:

I married the wrong person.

He should make me feel loved.

There is someone else better out there.

I believed those lies. They started to weave a tangled web of confusion in my heart. All I could see was all that was wrong with him. I became so blind to his good. I became so blind to my not-so-good.

TerKeurst said that's when she heard a statement that grabbed her: "Love isn't a feeling, it's a decision."

She went home and flipped to 1 Corinthians 13. This time, instead of reading it like a list of how love should make her feel, she read it as if she could decide to make her love fit these qualities. She boldly declared over her marriage, "My love *will* be kind. My love

> *"A strong marriage requires two people who choose to love each other even on those days when they struggle to like each other."*
>
> *- Dave Willis*

will be patient. My love *will* persevere. Not because I feel it—but because I choose it."

Slowly, the cold, stone wall between her and her husband started to come down.

"It wasn't easy. It wasn't overnight. But slowly," she says, "our attitudes and actions toward one another changed."

And she stopped *believing* the marriage lies and *replaced* them with three marriage truths:

Having a good marriage is more about being the right partner than having the right partner.

Love is a decision.

The grass isn't greener on the other side. It's greener where you water and fertilize it.

The e-mail ended with this sweet note of encouragement:

Maybe you've heard the marriage lies before. Maybe you're hearing them right now.

My heart aches for you if you are in a hard place in your marriage. And believe me, I know tough relationships are stinkin' complicated and way beyond what a simple devotion can possibly untangle. But maybe something I've said today can help loosen one knot . . . or at least breathe a little hope into your life today.

Talk about *things I wish I knew*! I heard and believed each of these lies so clearly in my first marriage that it drove me to search for a reprieve outside of it. I convinced myself that because Alex was not living up to his end of the bargain in meeting my needs, I was justified in satisfying them elsewhere. Remember the guy I was going to run away to Italy with? The end of that affair wreaked extra emotional fallout I had to deal with, because not only was I unloved by my husband, but my substitute love had left me as well. And it caused even more lies to pop up while I was considering remarriage. Things like: "You can't be faithful." "No one can make you happy." And, "If anyone knew the truth, they'd leave you."

Thank God I learned that those were lies and replaced them with the same truths Lysa mentioned. Love is a decision, so it doesn't matter that no human can make me happy. I will choose to make myself happy, and I will choose to be faithful.

And by reading other people's stories, I learned it was okay to share my truth.

In fact, I read about one couple who had had an affair with each other—they had each been married to other people when they met and began their relationship—and today they were running a successful marriage ministry. Obviously they had quite a bit of fallout to deal with themselves; it wasn't all roses and sunshine. There was more than a decade of dark, nasty transition and recovery time, but it gave me so much hope. Praise God! If they can do *that* and God can bless them with a ministry, surely I can still find a decent guy, be happy, and still be used for a purpose.

The Four Horsemen

What often happens in our marriages is we feel disappointed or disenchanted when our expectations of the person or the relationship don't measure up to reality. We start criticizing the other person as if it's their fault, and eventually that criticism, coupled with disappointment, evolves into contempt for them.

In *The Seven Principles for Making Marriage Work*, John Gottman goes into great depth about the four signs by which he can predict, with astounding accuracy, whether or not a couple will get divorced. "Certain kinds of negativity, if allowed to run rampant, are so lethal to a relationship that I call them the Four Horseman of the Apocalypse," Gottman says. "Usually these horseman clip-clop into the heart of a marriage in the following order: criticism, contempt, defensiveness and stonewalling."[19]

Contempt is defined as "disapproval tinged with disgust, disdain, a feeling that a person or thing is beneath one's dignity and unworthy of one's notice, respect, or concern. The state of being despised; dishonored; disgraced.[20]" Wow! Just reading that definition made me cringe! I realized that's exactly what I felt toward my ex-husband.

Once you pass that thresh-old of being disappointed in something your spouse does to being disappointed in *who he or she is* as a person, contempt develops, and it's really hard to

> *"Feelings are just visitors, let them come and go."*
>
> *- Mooji*

come back from, though it's not impossible. You have to make a conscious decision to believe the best in the other person and control yourself from living in a state of offense, but it is very difficult. It's part of that love decision. Choosing to act or react in a certain way, regardless of the way you *feel*. It's choosing to see your spouse in the best light, with pure motives and intentions, rather than assuming your spouse is constantly hurting or disappointing you intentionally. Once you live in that mind-set, you eventually shut down, because what's the use? And that's when the other two horsemen of defensiveness and stonewalling come charging into the battlefield.

Many of the books recommended at the end of this chapter and the previous one can help you put safeguards for your relationship into motion, make you aware of things to watch for and be cognizant of, to keep you from getting to this place. Gottman's book is a good start.

A Dream Is a Wish Your Heart Makes—Isn't it?

In the six months between our engagement and our wedding, I started having the craziest dreams. Every night.

I'm sure many anxious brides have experienced the same things: missing the bus to the wedding site, forgetting things for the ceremony, etc. And I even had some stranger, seemingly unrelated nightmares: tornadoes, floods, natural disasters . . . not even necessarily things to do with the wedding day.

Then, mixed in all of that, there were the dreams that were embarrassingly intimate and passionate. Ones I couldn't share with my fiancé for fear of making him feel jealous or question my loyalty. I dreamed about my exes. Not all of them, just the "big" ones, my first love, my first serious boyfriend whom I thought I was going to marry; never my ex-husband, which I found interesting.

In each of my dreams, I was striving, struggling, aching to be with them, and them with me. We would run after each other, and every time we found ourselves alone, there was wholeness, peace. Just holding their hand or being in their embrace was a surge of ecstasy. But then something would drag us apart again.

In every dream, I was acutely aware that I was engaged to be married to Barry. And I was angry about it. He was keeping me from this ultimate state of euphoria with the other person. I knew *they* would make me happy, but I was already committed to him. Stuck. Trapped.

I would wake up, and those powerful emotions from my dreams would linger, sometimes for as long as an hour into the morning. The yearning to be with the other person, the outrage of the unfairness and the bitterness toward Barry. In my waking state, there were even the additional feelings of guilt for wanting these things to be true and real, and knowing how unfair that was to Barry. Sometimes the dreams were so real I would wake up crying, thinking my infidelity had actually happened; that he would be crushed and never forgive me.

But each day, as the sleep eventually wore off and more coherent thoughts prevailed, I would realize I can't control my dreams. I had nothing for which to feel guilty. And I don't want to be with those people anyway. My exes are my exes for a reason. There was a specific reason, or number of reasons, that caused us to go our separate ways; being with them again wouldn't change that fact. Besides, I was happy with Barry, not trapped.

In my lucid moments, I knew that was true and that the dream emotions were false. But that didn't make the dreams any less powerful, or confusing.

I wondered if my dreams were revealing my true inner feelings, telling me that deep down I wasn't really happy, that I was fooling myself. Which made me feel like a terrible person for going through with this relationship with Barry and our wedding. And it made me feel a little crazy. Was something wrong with me?

After weeks of intense, vivid, bizarre dreams night after night, I started doing some research to figure out what my subconscious was trying to tell me. I purchased a dream dictionary and searched many of the topics and recurring themes online.

Turns out, dreams about natural disasters like tornadoes and floods are indicative of high amounts of stress in your waking life or signs of major changes and the feelings of things spinning out of control. *Oh, like planning a destination wedding and honeymoon in six months*? Yeah, I think that may have been the trigger there.

Even more interestingly, everything I could find on dreaming about your exes said that these dreams do not mean you are still in love with or want to be with that person; they often simply imply you are subconsciously desiring what you had in that relationship that you are currently lacking. Here are some of the explanations I found:

• To see an old ex-boyfriend from childhood in your dream refers to a freer, less-encumbered relationship. The dream serves to bring you back to a time where the responsibilities of adulthood (or marriage) did not interfere with the spontaneity of romance. You need to recapture the excitement, freedom, and vitality of youth that is lacking in your present relationship.[21]

• Ex-lovers in a dream can often become a symbol of hope for love that may be currently missing in your waking life.

• Dreaming about an ex can be the subconscious minds way of remembering certain qualities that your ex possessed that your current relationship is missing. Maybe you had an ex-boyfriend that was extremely good with your family while your current boyfriend is cold toward others. Certain qualities and traits that are missing in your current relationship can often show up in a dream to fill this void. You may or may not have feelings for your ex, but usually people dream about certain qualities about an ex rather than an ex themselves.

• People who are often going through stressful times in their lives will often dream of a period of time when life was "more simple." Sometimes that period of time will be represented with an ex. When you are in an unsatisfying relationship, your subconscious will sometimes revisit a happier period of your life in a dream.[22]

• Dreaming about exes is very common—particularly when entering or leaving a relationship— because these are times when we're most vulnerable. We don't know where things are going, so our unconscious often goes into overdrive to help us establish firmer emotional ground. While some people feel guilty about it, especially if they're committed to someone else, it's really the mind's way of helping to heal and move on.[23]

Let your past be a place of reference.... not a place of residence

All of this hit the nail on the head. On top of the obvious stress and anxiety of the major transition in my life at that time, I already knew I was feeling a lack of intimacy and passion in our relationship. Those were not things I had dealt with in these other relationships because I'd never gotten to a point of experiencing the day-in and day-out of real everyday life with these other guys.

One website even said, "It's a fallacy that dreams capture unconscious thoughts—dreams represent thoughts that we are all too aware of. A typical dream would translate into the types of thoughts that we might write down in a diary or tell a best friend. Dreams represent your key thoughts which pinpoint the problems right now."[24]

Why do I tell you all of this very private and somewhat embarrassing information? In case you are reading this and you have been having dreams or fantasies about your exes and are wondering, *What if?*

I know much of this is out of your control, but in your waking hours, don't fret and wonder if something is wrong with you. There isn't. A dream may be a wish your heart makes, but look for the ways you can make it come true in reality when you're wide-awake, with your

> If you carry bricks from your past relationship to the new one you will build the same house.

eyes wide open. Don't dwell on anything that *could have* been. You can drive yourself crazy for the rest of your life with shoulda, coulda, woulda. I'll say it again, your exes are your exes for a reason. Leave them where they belong, in your past. And focus on ways to incorporate solutions for those unsatisfied longings in your present relationship.

The Invisible Bond

Speaking of exes, several of the books I studied leading up to our wedding recommended *The Invisible Bond* by Barbara Wilson.

I ordered it, but didn't really feel the need to read it since I *only* had one other short-lived sexual partner other than my first husband. I really didn't think "soul ties," as they are referred to in many other books and circles, were something I struggled with. I figured I would read it at some point to understand and help other people who might come to me and need help dealing with those things.

However, on our wedding night, the stifling feelings I had had with Barry before our premarital sexual fast were still there. I thought after we got married those negative emotions would go away and lovemaking would be as wonderful as it had been in the beginning.

But much to my dismay, nothing changed when we said "I do." On our wedding night, the sex felt just as bland and obligatory as it had become before. And I *hated* myself for it. I wanted our intimate life to be rich and passionate and delightful. But it was more like, *Well, we're married now, better get a quickie in before our reception dinner because I know I'm going to be too tired afterward.* The honeymoon was much of the same.

I could not understand why I wasn't hungry for him, or for sex at all. What was wrong with me?

I apologized so many times on our honeymoon for just "not being in the mood" and letting him down. I was frustrated and angry with myself and very, *very* confused. Since I thought God had taken away my fleshly desires before our marriage, I thought He would just give them back afterward. But it wasn't quite that simple.

Invisible bonds, but not inconsequential.

God love my sweet husband for enduring all my baggage and mess and still loving me while I charted these turbulent and confusing waters. I cracked open the first page of Wilson's book once we were home from our honeymoon, and before I had even finished the introduction, I *knew* I needed her message.

She started the book with a checklist of the earmarks of a

bonded heart. I found myself circling almost every single one. Things like:

> If you waited for marriage to have sex, but then later divorced, did you become promiscuous prior to your second marriage?

> You may be in a committed, loving marriage relationship right now, but when you make love do the faces of past lovers sometimes flash through your mind? Do you find yourself comparing your spouse's lovemaking abilities with others from the past?

> Do you often find yourself fantasizing about past lovers: *what if I had married him or her instead*?

> Have you married for a second or third time only to find history repeating itself? *What is wrong with me?* you ask. *Why can't I pick the right one*?

> Did you enjoy sex before you were married, but now it's not so exciting? Or do you have to conjure up pornographic images to become aroused before lovemaking?

> Do you find that even though you're married you can't resist flirting with members of the opposite sex and desiring their attention?

I felt so exposed. It was as if Barbara Wilson were sitting inside my head, scrolling through my thoughts, asking me these very private questions that I would never admit to myself or another living soul.

What I didn't understand prior to this was that I didn't have to have intercourse with someone to have emotionally or physically bonded myself to them. And that even though my first sexual partner was my first husband, and *within* our marriage, there were still pieces of me that were tied to him that needed to be loosed.

Wilson wrote,

So why make so much noise about sexual bonding? Why can't we simply leave the past behind?

That would be precisely the strategy I would recommend if not for the fact that these invisible bonds from the past continue to exercise profound influence in the present. Sexual bonding has the potential to radically alter your view of yourself, of others, and of sex. It can propel you along a destructive course of promiscuity and other high-risk behaviors. It can impair your ability to choose healthy people to date and marry. It can lead to sexual addiction or sexual dysfunction. And it can affect your ability to have close, intimate relationships with others and God…

…If you find these words speaking to you, you're not alone. As I speak to teens and young adults, and as I work closely with hurting men and women, I hear the same stories thousands of times over. There isn't anything you could tell me right now I haven't heard from countless others. One after the other, in hesitant, broken words laden with shame and fear, people recount to me their sad, hidden secrets. I hear it all—more than I could ever have imagined.

And God hears it too. He hears all the anguished cries of hurting people like you. He empathizes with your pain and struggles. He sees your broken heart. He feels your wounds. And He knows the rocky path you walk every day.

Not only does He hear, but He also offers hope, help and answers. His heart breaks with yours and He holds out hands of love, grace, mercy, forgiveness, healing, peace, rest, joy and compassion. He promises to renew, restore, rebuild and reward. He's done it for me. For years I tried fixing myself, but nothing worked...

...The greatest miracle of all is the absence of [my] shame.[25]

If any of that resonates with you, I recommend you grab a copy of Wilson's book for yourself and go on the same journey I did. Untie your heart and walk into the freedom of bondage from your past.

Ebb and Flow

The following words from Anne Morrow Lindbergh's *Gifts from the Sea* sums up the ever-changing feelings in our marriages:

> When you love someone you do not love them all the time, in exactly the same way, from moment to moment. It's an impossibility. It's a lie to even pretend to. And yet this is exactly what most of us demand. We have so little faith in the ebb and flow of life, of love, of relationships. We leap at the flow of the tide and resist in terror of its ebb. We are afraid it will never return. We insist on permanency, on duration, on continuity; when the only continuity possible, in life as in love, is in growth, in fluidity—in freedom.[26]

These words gave me such a clear visual understanding. I pictured a little girl playing in the surf, enjoying the high tide, and then running after the waves as they pulled back, as if they were gone forever. How silly? As adults we know the water will surge back again. Why do we find it so difficult to see the same is true with our emotions in our marriages?

The more I read, the more my perspective on the purpose and meaning of marriage shifted drastically. I began to piece together that the reason I was so unhappy in my first marriage was because I was counting on my marriage and my husband to make me happy. I was trying to make him happy as well, but that's pretty hard to do when you're walking around miserable, unhappy, and unsatisfied yourself!

I realized that marriage isn't about being happy at all. And if you're planning on marrying someone *because* they make you happy, you're in for a huge disappointment. Only you can make yourself happy by focusing on the right things in life, which starts with your own well-being. In fact, I'll take

BE ~~WITH~~ SOMEONE WHO MAKES YOU HAPPY

it a step further and tell you that happiness should not even be your goal. Happiness is always fleeting, merely a passing emotion. What we should all really be focusing on developing is True Joy. If you're not sure you know the distinction, check out Kay Warren's book *Choose Joy Because Happiness Isn't Enough*.

Warren gets right to the point: "In case you haven't figured it out by now, let me share a secret with you: Nobody's going to take care of you. I don't mean that in a cynical way. I don't mean that in a bash-on-husband, bash-on-boyfriend, bash-on-parents, bash-on-children way. I just mean that at the end of the day no one is going to see to these three aspects of your life: physical, emotional and spiritual."[27]

Lysa TerKeurst, author and founder of Proverbs[31] Ministries, shared this story online:

Recently, I had dinner with a twenty-nine-year-old friend who would love to be married.

I shared with my friend that when I was single, I thought marriage was all about finding the right partner. I think it's good to have a list of standards we look for in a spouse. However, it can never be with the expectation that if I find that special someone, they'll right all my wrongs and fill up all my insecurities.

To expect another person to make me feel happy, secure and fulfilled will leave me disappointed at best and disillusioned at worst. *Even a great spouse makes a very poor God.*

So my friend decided instead of just focusing on finding the right partner, she would let God work on her heart to help her become the right partner.[28]

How much more plainly could I receive the answers to all the questions that were overwhelming me?

"The List"

When I was sixteen, some well-meaning mentors of mine recommended I make a list of the things I absolutely wanted in my husband, from physical attributes to character traits. Four typed pages and 160 bullet points later, I had what a "perfect spouse" looked like to me down on paper. Things like: "two to five years older than me, 5'8" to 6'2" tall, dark-colored, moderately short styled hair, nice abs, no visible tattoos or piercings, strong Christian example and leader (or striving to become),

> *"Marriage is not as much about finding the right person as it is being the right person."*
>
> *- John Bevere*

passionate with a clear, concise dream/goal/calling, makes me laugh, takes me on picnics, notices and remembers 'the little things'". . . You get the point. Some valid, some negligible, some ridiculously adolescent.

This exercise did make it very easy for me to date. As soon as I saw something in someone that was a nonnegotiable on my list, I would walk away from him before I got emotionally attached or invested. *He didn't make it through the filter*, I told myself.

The negative part of this exercise was that it taught me to look for the imperfections in every potential suitor I met, without considering my own shortcomings. And to keep seeking an imaginary person who did not exist.

"In the history of the universe, there has been only one perfect person. He remained single all his life and died young. The rest of us are imperfect creatures, deeply flawed, struggling to find our way through the complex maze of relationships and choices we encounter. We make mistakes, we learn and grow, we adapt and move on."[29] David and Lisa Frisbie began their book *Happily Remarried* with this poignant thought.

Barry and I chose to open our wedding ceremony with the same quote because it is such a paradigm shift on how to look for a marriage partner. When you begin with this foundational building block in mind—that we are all flawed—then you seek a spouse and maintain your relationship with an unprecedented level of grace. Knowing that no one is going to be perfect, when your partner misses the mark, it's okay. It does not mean they are defective and you must now walk away, or if you are already married that you have to live with the miserable knowledge that you chose the "wrong one."

Omartian offered some additional advice on this:

> I think if I could help a new wife in any area, it would be to discourage her from coming into her marriage with a big list of expectations and then being upset when her husband doesn't live up to them. Of course there are some basics that should be agreed upon before the wedding date such as fidelity, financial support, honesty, kindness, basic decency, high moral standards, physical and emotional love and protection. When you don't get those things, you can ask for them. When you still don't get them, you can pray for them. But when it comes to specifics, you can't require one person to meet all of your needs. The pressure to do that and fulfill your dreams at the same time can be overwhelming to a man.

> If we try to control our husbands by having a big list for them to live up to and then are angry and disappointed

when they can't, we are the ones in error.[30]

The Parrotts quote a divorce attorney who once told them the number one reason two people split up is because they "refuse to admit they are married to a *human being*."

"In every marriage, mutual hope gives way to mutual disillusionment the moment you realize your partner is not the perfect person you thought you married. But then again, he can't be. No human being can fill our idealized dreams. A let down is inevitable," they said.31

The remedy for all of this is keeping the right mind-set and realistic expectations going in to marriage. But don't take my word for it, I'm not the expert. I recommend delving further into the methods and advice these authors offer on how to do this in the books at the end of this chapter.

The Greatest Romance

A few months ago I heard a story of an executive who quit his $100 million salary job after receiving a note from his young daughter listing twenty-two recent milestones he had missed in her life.

When I posted the story on my Facebook page, I had an overwhelming response—but mostly from women. I think men felt convicted by the story. But for women, it struck the deepest cord in their soul's desire to be pursued, sought after, fought for. Having a father who would forsake his wealth, or even his whole life, to be with them is a desire that is woven into every single one of us. And there's a reason it's there.

There are many great books that explain this more eloquently than I ever could. One of the best I ever read was *Captivating* by Stasi Eldredge. In it she explains how we were created and built for this romance. To be pursued. Not by a human man on earth, but by the lover of our souls, Jesus Christ.

This year I read a book called *Redeeming Love* by Francine Rivers. It's a creative retelling of the story of Hosea and his prostitute wife, Gomer, from the Bible, which is one big metaphor for Christ's love for us. Boy, will that story change your life! I absolutely could not put it down.

Gomer, in her feelings of filth and unworthiness, kept running back to her old life of other men and abuse. She couldn't even begin to imagine that any man could want her for anything other than her body, her beauty, what she could give them. But Hosea was driven by his relentless, unconditional love for her. No matter how many times she ran away, he went back for her, again and again and again.

Hosea is literally known as the "Prophet of Divine Love," because he demonstrated the exact kind of supernatural love that only Jesus can have for us. Tears streamed down my face and my heart raced more than any romance novel could

provoke as I read of this one man's devotion to his wife. Because my soul cries out for the same ceaseless pursuit, despite my own filth. It's beautiful.

Falling into this romance for myself is what allowed me to take the pressure off Barry to be my perfect lover. And gives me the freedom of knowing it's not my responsibility to be everything to him either. We simply get to share our journey together, enjoying each other's company, strengths, and insights as we continue to work on ourselves and on the mission God has for us on this earth.

Fathers, Be Good to Your Daughters

My father has exemplified what it means to be a Christian man, husband, brother, son, and father every day of my life. I have never seen him waver. The strength and conviction of his character inspires those around him to be better themselves.

I have watched him lead our immediate (and extended family at times) spiritually. I have seen him confidently assume leadership roles in church my whole life. He is always smiling and laughing. His countenance creates joy in every person he encounters. You just feel better after being around my father.

His love is unconditional, even when I have done things to disappoint him.

He loved me enough to discipline me when I was younger, but would always hold me in his arms while I cried afterward. Still today when I miss the mark, he wraps me in his arms and tells me, "It's okay," and I know he still loves me anyway.

My father has a servant's heart and is a true gentleman. He is always the first to open a door, lift heavy things, fix any and everything for anyone, give someone a ride, deliver a meal, and sow money generously. I have seen him go out of his way at his inconvenience to help people in need. I have watched him pray for and with people, visit people in the hospital, deliver communion to people who were shut in, minister to hurting souls, and baptize those in need. He truly loves people with all his heart.

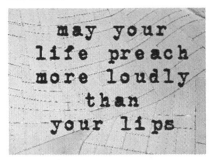

may your life preach more loudly than your lips

I never had to look past my father for an example. And I pray that I can emulate his example to the people in my life.

My father has tried every day of my existence to show me the love of our heavenly Father. And he has succeeded, as much as humanly possible. It is so easy for me to read about the character of God and believe it because I have lived with a glimpse of it my whole life here on Earth.

I would say I'm biased, but anyone who has ever met my father knows every word of this is true. I have had multiple people reach out to me to tell me what my father has done for them and meant to them. I know his brothers are more of the same and I am so fortunate to call the Pennington men my family.

I am blessed beyond measure to call Donald my daddy.

With such an incredible example and standard of what a "real man" should be in my life, sometimes it's easy for me to expect too much from other men. I remember the times I shouted at my ex-husband for not doing something the way my father would or for doing something he would never do.

I will never forget the advice my mom gave me once when I was comparing my ex to what a "real man" should be. She sweetly reminded me that my father has had a lot more practice at being a great man. He spent his whole life becoming "mister perfect"; he didn't start out that way, and it's not really fair to expect that from a newlywed husband.

What wisdom from a woman who spent her whole life covering any faults my father may have had from her children and guarding his reputation so we always had the best perspective of our father! She knew you can't follow someone you don't respect.

This is not about "settling" for someone; it's about acknowledging that you are both flawed individuals who need grace. With Barry, I try to live with much more patience and grace and the sweet expectancy that one day my child will get to experience having a father like my own.

But this will only happen if I continue to help draw that out of him by loving and respecting him unconditionally, just as he is, every step of the way. This is not going to occur if I am constantly reminding him all the ways he doesn't measure up to Donald. I must allow him to be secure in the freedom to be who he is while he's working to become better.

Pastor Brian Tome said,

After being married for more than twenty years, doing countless premarital and marital counseling sessions, and interacting with hundreds of other couples who are either happily or unhappily married, I now realize that while spiritual alignment and sexual chemistry are important, neither makes for a happy married life.

What's the key ingredient above and beyond all these things? Being married to a person who is focused on your freedom...

...I have a great life in large part because I have a woman who cheers me on and fights for my freedom. She encourages me to dream big visions, to bite off big projects and to be fearless in stepping out in faith...

...You don't have to encourage your spouse in the same way that Libby encourages me. But you need to encourage him or her in some way toward freedom. And if you are dating someone who isn't cheering you on to broad pastures, end it. They need to grow significantly or the rest of your life will be stifled.[32]

The Secret Ingredient

At the end of their book *Men Are Like Waffles, Women Are Like Spaghetti,* Bill and Pam Farrell wrap up their teaching and advice with The Secret Ingredient:

The secret ingredient is always that special something that makes the food taste so good—so out of the ordinary. When people sense that there's something special in a recipe, they probe a little further and ask, 'Hey! What's in this?' We have been asked that question for over 21 years. People have asked us how we stay in love, how our love stays fresh and strong. People ask us for the secret ingredient all the time.

That special something in our relationship is simply the grace and strength we receive from our relationship with God. This ingredient really isn't too secret because He wants all of us to know Him and the plan He has for our lives as husband and wife...

> "He loves us not because we are loaveable but because HE IS LOVE.".."
>
> - CS Lewis

...[We] have seen in our own life, and in the lives of countless other marriages, that the source and strength to love springs from the love God first gives us. We sign all of our books with the same verse that was etched into the wedding gifts we gave each other: *We love because He first loved us* (1 John 4:19).

Ecclesiastes 4:12 explains this source of strength: "Though one may be overpowered, two can defend themselves. But, a cord of three strands is not quickly broken."[33]

December 8th, 2013

Our wedding day had finally arrived – it was a stunning 80 degrees and sunny with a perfect Bahamian breeze. As our ship ported into Nassau, our wedding site was already being prepared a thirty minute shuttle ride from the dock. I wouldn't see Barry until I arrived on-site just before our ceremony, he slept in our officiant-friend's stateroom the night before. I spent the morning pampering, primping, photoshooting and dancing, of course, with my sister and soon-to-be sister-in-law.

There were no more butterflies, or stomach knots, or anxious uncertainty; there was no more fear or panic. There was only peace, and a calm excitement for the day, and life, ahead. I felt completely and utterly prepared, more than I ever imagined I could have; especially given my freakout over our engagement a mere six months prior. So much had transpired in those six months (more on that in the chapters ahead).

What We Learned

During those preparatory months, I became so convicted about the misconceptions we all walk into marriage with that I wanted our wedding ceremony to be a stark reminder of what marriage is really about. I wanted Barry and I to be going into it with the proper mind-set and expectations, and I wanted to use our ceremony as a time to show our friends and family what we had learned.

We dedicated a segment of our ceremony to this very thing, and we both prepared a statement about what each of us had taken away from our marriage-preparation process to read aloud.

I actually left my notes in my room that morning, so I winged my speech. On our shuttle ride from the port to our beach site, my sister teased, "If it's not in your heart, you didn't really learn it." I don't remember exactly what I said, but it was the gist of what I had written beforehand. Shouting over the crashing waves that afternoon, I shared:

> Immediately after Barry and I got engaged, I had a crisis moment. I knew I loved Barry with my whole heart and we had already decided to spend the rest of our lives together, but why did we have to be married? What is marriage really for? Why does it exist? I really wanted to understand God's purpose for marriage because I felt, at the time, like I didn't at all. I thought, *We are perfectly happy living our lives the way we are, why did we have to*

go and ruin it by getting married? I was nervous and terrified and confused and questioned whether I could succeed in marriage.

I definitely knew what all *doesn't* make a marriage work, but I wasn't so sure I understood what would make it work.

So I set out on a journey. To get the answers to all those questions.

I had heard my whole life in youth group, church, and camp, you need to "have God at the center of your relationship for it to succeed." But what the heck does that really mean? In real everyday life?

I still don't have all the answers, but over the last six months, I've read more than a dozen books, weekly met with a therapist, completed a premarital course with Barry, and had one very insightful conversation with Jennifer Beckham, one of my heroes and mentors who is a Christian author, minister and public speaker.

I believe the answer to having "God at the center of your relationship" is two-fold.

First, it means that Barry is not my source. He cannot be. It's not even his job to be. It is physically humanly impossible for him to do everything and be everything I need to be happy on a day-to-day basis. To expect that of him is only to set him up for failure and to set myself up for disappointment. But thankfully, in the words of Kirk Franklin, "there is a lover named Jesus!" and *He is* able to do all of those things. And as long as I turn to Him for my strength and joy and peace and happiness, I take the

"We love because He first loved us."

- 1ˢᵗ John 4:19

pressure off Bear to be my everything. So even when my proverbial "love tank" is running low, I can get it filled from a higher source, and when my love tank is full, I'm able to pour my love back out to other people, especially Barry.

Second, I think this concept of having God at the center of your marriage means living out Christ-like behavior and attitudes every day in your marriage. *Unconditionally* loving your spouse and offering them grace, even when they are at their ugliest. Despite all their frustrating personality flaws, their quirks, their mood swings, and their bad days, and even when they hurt you, it's loving them anyway. It's seeing them for the beautiful creation they are, seeing what they can and will be, rather than how they are acting at the moment. And that's WAY easier said than done!

But it goes back to being filled up by God first. I can only do that if I get filled up with God's love first. That's why we picked 1 John 4:9–11 as the theme for today, "We [are able to] love *because* [and only because] He first loved us." That's the whole point.

Jennifer Beckham explained it to me this way: "We are not in marriage for ourselves, for our happiness. It's not about us. We are put in a marriage with the person we are to literally build that person, to encourage them, to bless them, to love them into the full picture of the person they were created and designed by God to be. And when they hurt you, you go back to God to get healed, filled up, and you go back in again." Endlessly.

The only way I've found for me to do that is reminding myself every time I get hurt or disappointed by Barry, that I, too, am imperfect. And I need grace. Remembering that I make mistakes and hurt people. That I hurt and disappoint God. But when I do, every time—*every* single time—without exception, no matter how far I went or how wrong I was, He invites me lovingly back into His arms with grace. Passionate grace. More than that, when I am running away from Him in my actions and deeds, He chases after me! That's love.

And I believe what we are called to do is to exemplify that love back into our marriages.

So there it is. The summation of what I learned is that to make marriage work, you've got to set realistic expectations for yourself and your partner and be mindful of where you are seeking your fulfillment. The reason we end up so unhappy and bitter and disenchanted in marriage is because we focus on deriving our happiness *from* the marriage. We expect perfect, fairy-tale love from a person who cannot give it to us. When we shift our focus to the True Source of Joy, and run to Him every time we encounter a disappointment, everything falls into place. When you enter marriage knowing all of this up front, the pressure is off and everyone wins. Individually joyful people live joyful marriages.

After Happily Ever After

Lysa TerKeurst told a story about her own lessons from after the ride into the sunset:

> I was cleaning my kitchen counter the other day and brushed past a framed snapshot taken on my wedding day.
>
> I stared at the photo taken 22 years ago. I laughed at how big my hair was. I sighed at how much smaller my waist was. And I wished I could pull that young bride aside and give her some advice and perspective that would certainly

have benefitted me.

I would have whispered . . .

"Sweetheart, there is only one day where marriage naturally looks like the storybooks. It's this day. This day, your wedding day, is where every hour has been arranged and planned to be beautiful and special. And as you wave goodbye to

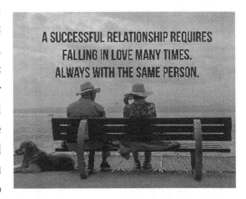

this one day, realize what happens from here is all about choices.

Choose to understand that love isn't always a feeling. Many days love will be a choice. It's a choice to press through and learn to enjoy the fragile blend of both the bliss and disappointments of two people learning to become a family.

Being married is amazing. Being married is incredibly difficult. Being married can seem impossibly hard. Being married can seem incredibly beautiful. There is no other person who can frustrate me the way my husband can. There is no other person who can make me feel as loved as my husband can.

Yes, marriage is a fragile blend of all this and more.

Watch for these kinds of disillusioning thoughts and capture them before they take root:

'He didn't load the dishwasher even after I asked him to. He doesn't listen to me.'

'He just handed me a brochure about the new gym opening down the street. I'm never good enough for him.'

'He took a phone call while we're on date night. He doesn't love me enough to give me his full attention.'

Yes, the unraveling places of relationships often occur in these kinds of spots with these kinds of thoughts where little discouragements grow into big wedges of discontentment.

Thinking, talking, complaining and working on those things is not at all the same as praying for them.'"[34]

Final Food for Thought

Dear one, let me ask you, what kind of fairy-tale myths have you been believing about your life that have been setting you up for disappointment? This doesn't even necessarily have to be about relationships. Is there a dream or goal in your life that hasn't gone exactly the way you planned it and you're starting to feel disenchanted?

Jennifer Beckham talks much about this in her book *Get Over Yourself*. Her lifelong dream was to be a Disney princess—like, in real life. But as she found herself sitting on top of that pumpkin carriage float in the Main Street Electrical Parade waving to the crowd, she realized the disheartening truth that she still felt empty inside. Even accomplishing her biggest dream had left her feeling like something was missing. You might even call that her "Now What?" moment. She had to learn some of the same lessons I'll talk about in chapter 9 on her way to finding her true purpose.

Stick with me, we're just getting to the good stuff!

Recommended Books for

Chapter Seven

As I prepared for my second marriage, it was important for me to understand that what I was thinking and feeling was normal. That I was not a weirdo, I was not crazy, and I was not alone. These books helped me do that.

- *The New Rules for Love, Sex & Dating* by Andy Stanley
- *Things I Wish I'd Known Before We Got Married* by Gary Chapman
- *Second Marriage* by Richard B. Stuart
- *The Seven Principles for Making Marriage Work* by John C. Gottman
  Gottman takes a very scientific approach to love and marriage and it's very insightful.
- *The Power of a Praying Wife* by Stormie Omartian
  My mom gave me this book when I was seventeen and in my first serious relationship. I have read it several times now, at many different phases of my life. It gets more special, and more relevant, every time. It makes a great devotional study because there are thirty chapters that you can break up and study each day for a month.
- *Redeeming Love* by Francine Rivers
  The most passionate romance novel you will ever read!
- *Men Are Like Waffles, Women Are Like Spaghetti* by Bill and Pam Farrell

It's so important to understand our innate differences, and the Farrells present the information in a humorous and memorable format.

- *The Invisible Bond* by Barbara Wilson
- *Untangle: Break Wrong Soul Ties and Pursue Your Purpose* by Terri Savelle Foy
- *Crazy Good Sex* by Les and Leslie Parrott

Chapter Eight

"Before you ever get a problem God has already got your deliverance planned."

- Joyce Meyer

The Big Show
Sometimes God Doesn't Even Try to Be Inconspicuous

"A real friend is not the one who comes along next to you in your moment of weakness saying, 'yeah, you're right,' but the one who reminds you of the things you know in your moments of clarity that you just can't remember right now."
—Jennifer Beckham

My friend Charlene wasn't the only person I used as an interim therapist after my engagement. I also had a very timely conversation with Jennifer Beckham over lunch one day. (How I became friends with this real-life hero of mine is an incredible God-orchestrated story, you'll get to hear about it in the next chapter!) I told her about my freak-out after Barry proposed to me and our plan to move forward.

Then she asked me a very poignant question: "Do you feel like you've been released from your marriage with Alex?"

Ironically, I had just read Kenneth Hagin's *Marriage, Divorce and Remarriage*, which covered that topic, and had spent a great deal of time thinking through it. I explained that I absolutely believed I had been released from my marriage, but I wasn't sure when that had occurred. Was it sometime before Alex left, or when Alex left, or when our divorce was finalized?

That's when she told me the details of *her* story, well, the rest of it anyway. The part that picks up after her first book, *Get Over Yourself* when her and her husband's marriage hit their breaking point.

It Would Be So Much Easier If I Just Left!

Nine years into their marriage, just after she had released her first book, Jennifer's husband, Anthony, came to her and confessed he was battling a pornography addiction that had begun when he was a very young boy. Utterly defeated and with his walls down, he came with the desire for help and healing. "I'm glad you're free," He said, "Now I need to be free."

But, Jennifer was so hurt, so angry...Her initial reaction was not so flattering: "EXCUSE ME?! I'm going somewhere. I'm going to change the world. I don't have time for this." She begged God to let her leave. It was too painful to deal with, and she had a ministry to run and a world to change.

"It would be so much easier if I just left!" she screamed in frustration

But clearly heard God tell her to stay. In that moment, she felt the weight of the words that had just come out of her mouth, *I need to go change the world* but, here in her own house, there was a man hurting and broken, and she was about to walk out on him.

How often we do this? We are willing to give the best of ourselves to everyone else in the whole world, but often neglect the people in our own home. I once heard Joyce Meyer say something to the effect of, "You want a ministry? It starts in your own house, with your spouse, with your family. How dare we ask God to give us *other* people to love and bless and touch for Him, when we haven't even been good stewards of the ones he's already given us?" I'm not trying to put guilt and condemnation on you, I'm preaching to myself here!

This is another lesson I learned too late to save my first marriage, but you better believe it's something I am cognizant of and focus on now.

God did not release Jennifer from her marriage to Anthony, but instead used that season to teach her many invaluable lessons. He taught her about commitment. About grace. About loving someone through their pain, even when they are hurting you. Grievously.

(Please know I am not saying you should stay if you are being physically abused. If you feel your life or physical well-being is being seriously threatened, get yourself to a safe place. It's never okay to live with or inflict physical harm in a relationship. You can always let your partner receive help and/or reconcile while separated.)

> *"Love me when I least deserve it, because that's when I really need it."*
>
> - Swedish proverb

"That's the whole point of marriage," she said from the other side of our table at Panera that day. "It's not about love, or even about us. God puts us in a marriage with another person to heal them and them, us. To be His extension of love to them on this earth. It's the people who are nastiest and ugliest and meanest who need our love and grace and compassion the most. The saying, 'Hurting people hurt people' is true. It's about seeing them as a human being whom God created and loves regardless of how they are acting. And we are called to stay, and to love people, no matter what.

"And when they hurt us," she continued, "we go back to God to get filled up, to get healed, then we go back in. Over and over and over. Until they finally see we are not going anywhere. And it's safe. And they really start to heal and change. That's what marriage is about. So that's why I asked about your marriage to Alex." She paused.

"I do believe there are circumstances when God releases people from marriage, and that's between you and God, but at that point He is concerned with *how* we leave them. Do we leave them more broken and damaged and scarred than when we met them? Or do we leave them in a place of wholeness and freedom?"

The room was literally spinning. It was as if the world had been paused or muted. I couldn't hear the words Jennifer was saying anymore. I saw her lips moving, but all I could hear was the dread-laden voice in my mind coming to this terrifying realization: *Oh no. I left Alex in shambles. I destroyed him on my way out, probably on purpose. I have to have a conversation with him. I've got to tell him that even though our marriage was terrible and he wasn't anything near the person he wanted to be while in it, he can be now. I have to apologize to him.*

As quickly as those thoughts came up, they were countered with, *I have no way to reach him. He blocked my phone, deactivated his e-mail, blocked me on Facebook, and has moved multiple times. It is impossible for me to get in touch with him.* And just like that, the world resumed its pace, noise and color returned, and my eyes refocused on Jennifer, who had finished talking.

I asked the next gut-wrenching thought that entered my mind: "Do you think I'm supposed to leave Barry and get back with Alex to heal him?"

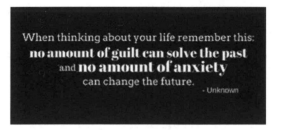

When thinking about your life remember this: **no amount of guilt can solve the past** and **no amount of anxiety** can change the future.
— Unknown

"Oh no. I don't think that at all. Because I don't believe God would do that to Barry."

Whew! My racing pulse slowed a little, but I still had some things to ponder. I decided I would pray about it and write a letter to Alex that I would *never* send, this was just going to be between me and God at this point.

But once I was back home, busyness resumed and I never got around to it. In fact, I kind of pushed the entire conversation out of my mind. That is, until six weeks later, when God smacked me right across the face with it.

The Apology

I was on a business trip when my phone rang for the second time with the same unknown number I had just sent to voice mail. Then I got a text message: "Can you call me when you get the time?"

Forgive people in your life, even those who are not sorry for their actions. Holding on to anger only hurts you, not them.

- Unknown

"I'm sorry, who is this? I'm about to run into an appointment."

"I understand, Rachel. This is your ex-husband, and given the opportunity, I'd like to talk to you."

I could barely maneuver my car into a parking spot at the first gas station I found as my stomach turned and my palms sweated and shook. Three and a half years. Three and a half years had passed since that day I came home from work to find his things gone and the note from his girlfriend on my table. I had only spoken to him twice since that day, about formalities.

Then I got this text.

Before I responded, I called Barry and thought aloud with him. "He is calling for one of two reasons: (a) he's calling to yell at me for continuing to stay in contact with 'his' family and friends, or (b) he's calling to apologize. But I really feel like he's calling to apologize."

Barry wasn't so sure, but agreed I should find out what he wanted.

I waited until I was through working that day and was back at my hotel to text Alex that he had permission to call me.

When he did, we spent about thirty minutes on the phone. He told me he had grown tired of not having me in his life—just as a positive influence—so he had gotten online the night before and had spent hours Facebook-stalking the last three years of my life. He saw our engagement and congratulated me. He said I deserved to be happy and that Barry seemed like a great guy. He asked how my parents and my brother were. Then he told me why he really called, which was to apologize. For everything.

He spent the next twenty minutes apologizing for hurting me, for leaving me, for the *way* he left, and then for ending our marriage. He apologized for letting someone else dictate how he treated someone he cared about. He apologized for being young and immature and being a stupid boy who hurt a wonderful woman. He apologized for making a spiritual and legal commitment to me but not being committed to *being in* a marriage.

He told me he had been so nervous about making the phone call, he had originally asked his sister to relay all these things for him.

Then he said the most freeing words I could have ever received: "Most importantly, I wanted to make sure *you* hadn't spent the last three years of your life thinking you could have done something differently to save our marriage. Thinking it was your fault. Yes, we both made mistakes, but I was the one who left in the first place, and I was the one who initiated the divorce and went through with it."

> *"Forgive others, not because they deserve forgiveness, but because you deserve peace."*
>
> *- Jonathan Lockwood Huie*

While the gravity of his statement was still setting in, I managed to get out, "Thank you." I told him I appreciated his apology and said, "I want you to know I have already forgiven you. I made that decision awhile ago. But there are some things I need to apologize to *you* for. Unfortunately, I will need some time to prepare that, so give me a couple weeks and I will likely write it in an e-mail to you."

He tried to tell me I didn't owe him any sort of apology, but I assured him that I most certainly did.

The following letter were the most heart-wrenching words I have ever penned in my life. I cried ferociously as the weight of every angry word I'd said and every hurtful deed I'd done to him washed over me, and as each thing went onto the paper, it was lifted away.

Alex,

I don't even know where to begin, but I keep getting some serious promptings to get this letter written to you so here we go.

First and foremost: in one text to me after our phone call you said that you are "eager to make your heart right as far as I go." I brought this up in counseling, and my therapist said that you don't owe me anything, except an apology, which you have provided. More than thoroughly! So don't think you have anything else to make up to me, or owe me.

Receiving your phone call was the single most healing thing that could have happened at that point in my life. Especially going into my marriage to Barry.

You said to me that you hoped I hadn't sat around the last three years blaming myself for our marriage ending and wondering if there was anything I could have done differently. Well, of course I have! Almost every day I have battled those thoughts. I felt like a failure.

I read in one book that women who experience divorce do tend to take on the identity of being "a failure," whereas men don't really experience that as much. That made me laugh.

I could send you the four pages of toxic thoughts I had about myself that I wrote in my journal after the disillusionment of our marriage. It's not pleasant. But I wrote them down to get them out of my head so they wouldn't be rattling around in there anymore. Things like: "No one wants you. You're not worth trying for. You messed up, this is what you have to deal with. You're too much to handle. You can't be in a serious relationship, you get bored too easily. You're damaged goods, who's going to want you now? You don't bring out the best in guys. You couldn't even make your marriage work, what makes you think you can lead a team or make an impact? You're a bad apple/influence, it's best if you're not around." And so on.

Even though I had gotten most of those thoughts out of my head in the last couple years, I still didn't have a great deal of confidence in whether I wanted to be married again, or if I even could.

The night Barry and I got engaged, I ordered about fifteen books on marriage, divorce, and remarriage, enrolled us in a premarital class, and started going to counseling for myself. I set out on a mission. I wanted to understand what God's purpose for marriage is, why it exists, and to make sure there was no emotional residue left from our marriage that I would be taking into mine and Barry's.

Then a series of events happened. As I began to learn about divorce and remarriage, I began to forgive myself for a lot of things. My biblical view on divorce was radically changed, and I learned about the circumstances when God releases you from marriage.

I sat down with Jennifer Beckham and had a very interesting conversation about the purpose of marriage— she taught me it's not about you, it's about building into another person. Loving them into who they were created to be. We also talked about how you leave a marriage. She said, "God may have released you from your marriage, but how did you leave? Did you leave contributing to that persons fears, doubts, insecurities and scars in life, or did you leave building them up?"

Immediately, I knew I needed to reach out to you and ask you for forgiveness for the way I left our marriage. But, as quickly as I was convicted of that, just as quickly the thought occurred to me that I had absolutely no way of contacting you. It was *exactly* six weeks later that you called me out of the blue.

So here we are, from the beginning:

I apologize for influencing/pressuring you to give up on your lifelong dream and leave the Navy for me.

I apologize for putting way too high of expectations on you and not giving you any room or grace to grow. For expecting perfection out of you, and for being so utterly and outwardly disappointed in you when you missed that mark.

I apologize for making you feel like you were never good enough.

I apologize for making your home a miserable place to come home to rather than your safe-haven, a place of peace and refreshment.

I apologize for being a hypocrite, every time I was.

I apologize for thinking I knew everything.

I apologize for all the disgusting things I said to you in anger.

I apologize for the time I hit you in the face with a copy of *1001 Ways to Be Romantic* (although you have to admit that is kind of funny in retrospect).

I apologize for every one of my bursts of temper.

I apologize for being immature and not being able to control myself or my emotions.

I apologize for being completely inflexible and never compromising with you.

I apologize for taking you for granted and letting myself get to a place of absolute contempt for you.

I apologize for adding to the pain, fear, and instability that was your childhood and life before I was in it.

I apologize for not having your back, every time.

I apologize for when I stopped being your best friend and put my allegiance elsewhere.

I apologize for disrespecting you, for not trusting you, or for never letting you take the lead.

I apologize for creating and contributing to such an environment that was not conducive or encouraging for growth, or peace, or love, or unity.

I apologize for giving up on you, and us.

I apologize for seeking the comfort, affection, and love I needed outside of our marriage. I see now how much pressure I put on you to fulfill something that was never your place anyway. I know now that I should have been turning to God to get filled up all those times I felt you were falling short and hurting me. That was not your fault. I should have had more faith, and patience. I should have given you the same unconditional love and grace that I have been afforded by Jesus. Although I am so thankful I was able to learn these things the hard way—as painful as it was and still is—so that I am now better prepared to bring out the best in Barry in our marriage.

I apologize for all the ways I was "religious."

I apologize for any way I pushed you further away from your own walk with God by giving you all kinds of false ideas of who He is and how He loves. It is *so* not like I "loved" you.

I apologize for every time I criticized you, judged you, or condemned you.

For all these things, and anything else I did not include, please forgive me.

You are an incredible man. When we met, you told me about the man you wanted to be, how you wanted to live, the things you wanted to do. And all the things you didn't want in life. Even though you may have fallen very far away from that image during our marriage, I need you to know that you can absolutely still be that man today, and more if you want. I can already see that you are moving in that direction.

> "Be the one who nurtures and builds. Be the one who has an understanding and a forgiving heart, one who looks for the best in people. Leave people better than you found them."
>
> - Marvin J. Ashton

You have such charisma and magnetism, people love being around you. You make people laugh and feel comfortable in their skin. You are an amazing friend, even when your friends are not-so-amazing to you. Don't ever lose that.

When you left, I was angry and numb. I couldn't process all that I was feeling at the time. A year later, the day I received our divorce paperwork in the mail, I cried and cried, and Barry held me. I told him I just didn't understand why you didn't want anything to do with me anymore. I understood that we weren't going to be married anymore—that we agreed on—but I couldn't understand how you could just flip a switch and stop being my friend. I told him, "Alex was my best friend. I'm not just losing my husband, I'm losing my best friend too. Why doesn't he want to be my friend anymore?"

And that was playing on my deepest hurts and insecurities of not being wanted. In your phone call you explained and apologized for that specifically, that you let someone else dictate how you treated me. Thank you for that. Those words healed the broken, gaping place in my heart.

Your phone call set me free. Gave me permission to trust myself again. To believe in myself. To accept our marriage for what it was: an irreplaceable learning experience to prepare me for the rest of my life, and especially for marriage in the future. A lesson in humility and grace. I have a compassion for other people, especially people who have or are going through divorce, that I never would have had I not gone through what I did with you and because of you. You have made me a better person.

You know in the marriage ceremony when the father "gives away" his daughter to her soon-to-be-husband? I wondered how this happens in second marriages, since the dad already gave her away. Well, our reconciliation feels a little like you giving me away to Barry. Giving me permission to go on and be happy. Thank you for letting me go, more healed and whole than I was three months ago.

Thank you again for your heartfelt, genuine, thoughtful apology. And thank you in advance for forgiving me.

I pray you all the best for the rest of your life.

I honestly didn't know what would happen after that. I didn't know if I would ever speak to him again or if that would be the end of it. Thankfully, that wasn't the end of the story. It got even better!

Alex replied to my letter in text saying,

Rachel, I don't know if this is the last I'll ever hear from you and I'll understand if it is, but I want you to know that it has been a long time since a tear has left my eye until today. The unbelievable love in that message for me as a human being [*I promise he used those exact words*] was breathtaking. I agree that *1001 Ways* to get smacked in the face was pretty funny and I provoked you. I missed you a lot in those three years of absence and I gave up on my best friend. Thank you again so so much for that message. I hope to keep you in my life no matter the capacity but will never put my desire for that to place friction between you and your future husband. With my whole heart I give you to Barry and would give you to him 1000 times if I had to.

> "THE TRUE MARK OF MATURITY IS WHEN SOMEBODY HURTS YOU AND YOU TRY TO UNDERSTAND THEIR SITUATION INSTEAD OF TRYING TO HURT THEM BACK."
> — ANONYMOUS

Wow. Now I get it. I could finally get past my own broken heart and wounded spirit to see that *this* is really what God's love looks like.

The next time I had dinner with Alex's sister, Kristine, she thanked me for taking his call and for sending him that letter. She recounted their conversation, saying, "He told me, 'Of all the decisions I've made in my life, good and bad, I know that marrying Rachel was a good decision if for nothing else than to learn what *true* forgiveness really means.'" [Goosebumps]

Yes, yes, yes! My letter had the exact outcome I had desired—to show Alex God's love in a way that surpasses human ability and understanding, for him to feel grace in a true and tangible way. To build him up and leave him better than I found him.

A month later I was able to walk into my marriage with Barry in total freedom. Restored. Healed. Whole. And confident that I finally understood how to love someone well. Knowing that I could bring out the best in someone and I *could* make a marriage work. I had closure, as they say in psychological circles.

But my heart was only in a place to receive Alex's phone call and his words to me *because* of the conversation I had with Jennifer weeks earlier. And the only reason I was able to understand and process the conversation with Jennifer was because of the books I was already reading and the growth I was already undergoing.

Everything was happening for a reason; it was all a well-laid, carefully executed plan that I was smack-dab in the middle of. When I looked back and saw all the dots connecting, I had to laugh. Sometimes God doesn't even try to be inconspicuous.

And the great news is, He's doing the exact same thing for you, right now. Even if you can't see it at this time.

I love what Steve Furtick says in *Crash the Chatterbox* when he talks about how it's easy for us to believe God will get us out of a mess that He has led us into. But our faith struggles with the belief that He will get us out of something we've gotten ourselves into, through bad decisions or rebelliousness.

> **What may seem like a Disappointment could be God setting you up for a rescue. Trust His Plan Even when you don't understand the path.**
> -Trent Shelton

Friend, I'm here to tell you, those are exactly the times when God loves to show up most! What an awesome display of His power that even when we screw up and veer off course and get ourselves into a mess, He is powerful enough still to get us out!

Trust Him. Let Him show up for you.

Restore [ri-stawr, -stohr]
Verb (used with object): restored, restoring.

1. to bring back into existence, use, or the like; reestablish: to restore order.

2. to bring back to a former, original, or normal condition, as a building, statue, or painting.

3. to bring back to a state of health, soundness, or vigor.

4. to put back to a former place, or to a former position, rank, etc.: to restore the king to his throne.

5. to give back; make return or restitution of (anything taken away or lost).

6. to reproduce or reconstruct (an ancient building, extinct animal, etc.) in the original state.

Synonyms

2. mend. See renew. 4. replace, reinstate. 6. rebuild.

Word Origin and History for restore

v. c.1300, "to give back," also, "to build up again, repair," from Old French restorer, from Latin restaurare "repair, rebuild, renew," from re- "back, again" (see re-) + -staurare, as in instaurare "restore," from PIE *stau-ro-, from root *sta- "to stand, set down, make or be firm," with derivatives meaning "place or thing that is standing". Related: Restored ; restoring.[35]

God is in the Restoration Business
He breathes life into lifeless places.

It doesn't matter if it's a relationship, your health, your

emotions, your dreams....

He brings dry bones out of the grave and wraps them in flesh once more.

He restores the years you lost, the love you lost, the friends you lost, the faith you lost, the dreams you lost, the opportunities you lost.   Over and above what we can even think of or imagine.

He makes all things new, again.

If you let Him.

If something in your life needs total restoration, read these promises below and be encouraged.

He CAN do it.

He HAS done it for others (including me).

He WANTS to do it for you.

"Behold, I am the Lord, the God of all flesh. Is anything too hard for me?" (Jeremiah 32:27, ESV)

"Be glad, O children of Zion, and rejoice in the Lord your God, for he has given the early rain for your vindication; he has poured down for you abundant rain, the early and the latter rain, as before. The threshing floors shall be full of grain; the vats shall overflow with wine and oil. **I will restore to you the years that the swarming locust has eaten, the hopper, the destroyer, and the cutter, my great army, which I sent among you. You shall eat in plenty and be satisfied, and praise the name of the Lord your God, who has dealt wondrously with you."** (Joel 2:23-26, ESV)

"See, I am doing a new thing! Now it springs up; do you not perceive it? I am making a way in the wilderness and streams in the wasteland." (Isaiah 43:19)

"Have mercy on me, O God, according to your steadfast love; according to your abundant mercy blot out my transgressions. Wash me thoroughly from my iniquity, and cleanse me from my sin! Behold, you delight in truth in the inward being, and you teach me wisdom in the secret heart. Purge me with hyssop, and I shall be clean; wash me, and I shall be whiter than snow. Let me hear joy and gladness; let the bones that you have broken rejoice. Hide your face from my sins, and blot out all my iniquities. Create in me a clean heart, O God, and renew a right spirit within me. Cast me not away from your presence, and take not your Holy Spirit from me. Restore to me the joy of your salvation, and uphold me with a willing spirit." (Psalm 51:1-2, 6-12, ESV)

"Return to your fortress, O prisoners of hope; even now I announce that I will restore twice as much to you." (Zechariah 9:12)

"Do you not know that your bodies are temples of the Holy Spirit, who is in you, whom you have received from God? You are not your own." (1 Corinthians 6:19)

"O God, hear my prayer and pleading. Restore your Temple, which has been destroyed; restore it so that everyone will know that you are God." (Daniel 9:17 GNT)

Amen.

Recommended Books for

Chapter Eight

- *Marriage, Divorce and Remarriage* by Kenneth C. Hagin
  This was a book I was afraid to read. Kenneth Hagin is a well-known and very influential American Pentecostal preacher. He is often referred to as the father of the "Word of Faith" movement. He served as the spiritual father to many of the ministries I had studied and followed for the last decade, which, at the time, were big on the Word, and not always big on grace. I was afraid his book would turn into a guilt-ridden spiritual reprimand saying that I couldn't be remarried, or I could only be divorced if my ex-husband was dead, an unbeliever, or had physically abused me. I was anticipating all the judgement and guilt I had perceived in my childhood church experience. I was blissfully delighted to find that Pastor Hagin "gets it." He talks about the law of love and grace we are called to. About how even Christians in marriage are still flawed people. There were some things still that challenged me, but because I had not felt condemned by his approach, I was able to receive them and grow.
- *Lineage of Grace* by Francine Rivers
  This is the story of five women in the lineage of Jesus who each had their own unique "Now What?" moments. And God showed up in each of their lives in big ways!
- *Bad Girls of the Bible* by Liz Curtis Higgs
  Sex. Scandal. Lies. These girls all had their skeletons, and God was about to use each of them for His purpose.

Chapter Nine

"The first to help you up are the ones who know how it feels to fall."

- Unknown

The Purpose for My Pain

"Someone in need is waiting on the other side of your obedience right now. There are people who need you to share what you have been through to help them get out of the mess they're in. YOU HAVE A STORY. You have a testimony. You have the wounds to prove that you've been through a tough time."
—*Terri Savelle Foy*

Crawling out of the pits in which we find ourselves is only half the battle. Once we are standing back on solid, sun-touched ground again and dust ourselves off, what's next? Do we continue down the path we were on before the pit? What if that path isn't an option anymore? Now what?

Restless

This is how I would describe myself six months after my honeymoon. Even though I had "recovered" from my divorce—I'd recognized my mistakes and flaws, apologized, received forgiveness and grace, learned, grown, and remarried—there was still a part of me that was broken, or at the least incomplete. Restlessly yearning for more.

Was getting emotionally and spiritually reconstructed and remarried really all there was to accomplish in my life? Or was there something more?

I questioned if there *could* be anything more. I felt like I was still too tainted. Like I had missed the chance to go after my full calling because of the mistakes I had made. I thought I had to settle for whatever I could get in life and like it. I imagined a life of menial work, of subpar fulfillment, a life of small dreams and accomplishments and daring not to ask for more.

Who was I to still think I could change the world? Or change my family's legacy? Or even make a dent in my community?

> Get your fire back. It's not over until God says it's over. Start believing again. Start dreaming again. Start pursuing what God put in your heart.
>
> - Joel Osteen

God had already blessed me and restored my life by bringing me a new husband, one who loved me unconditionally. One I could respect and be proud of. One who wakes up every day thinking of ways he can be better and ways he can make me happy. A peaceful and happy home of our own to come home to, and three beautiful, adoring animals. Wasn't that enough? Was I selfish to want more?

I had all but resigned myself to a life of complacency.

And I believe that is precisely what our enemy wants. If he can't destroy us by tearing our minds and hearts apart with a stream of toxic thoughts, at least he can convince us to settle and be satisfied with less than we were destined for. To not accomplish the fulfillment of our true purpose or use our God-given talents and abilities to the fullest extent.

Moves and countermoves. Our enemy is so skillful at deception, at distraction.

Dear friend, I'm here to tell you that God wanted more for me and He wants more for you.

Joel Osteen said, "You may be in a mess right now, it was your own fault, and you don't think there's anything good in your future. But God has you covered. He still wants you to accomplish your dreams."

Here's what I've learned about God. He doesn't just restore you, He always takes things a step further. "Now to Him [God] who is able to do far more abundantly beyond all that we ask or think *or can even imagine*, according to the power that works within us" (Ephesians 3:20 NASB, emphasis added).

Now, I have a pretty powerful imagination, but I have found it to be absolutely true that God will come up with things I never could even dream. And it's not because I'm special. He will do this for each of us, simply because that's who He is. He is good. He is love. And we are His children.

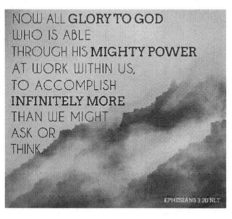

NOW ALL **GLORY TO GOD** WHO IS ABLE THROUGH HIS **MIGHTY POWER** AT WORK WITHIN US, TO ACCOMPLISH **INFINITELY MORE** THAN WE MIGHT ASK OR THINK.

EPHESIANS 3:20 NLT

In Matthew 7: 9-11, Jesus says, "You parents— if your children ask for a loaf of bread, do you give them a stone instead? Or if they ask for a fish, do you give them a snake? Of course not! So if you sinful people know how to give good gifts to your children, how much more will your heavenly Father give good gifts to those who ask Him."

I'm just finishing up Francine River's book *The Lineage of Grace*, which is about five women in the bloodline of Jesus. Each of them has a unique story about how God moved mountains in their lives not only to redeem the broken places but to bless them above and beyond what they could ever ask for, think of, or imagine.

I particularly love Bathsheba's story. Quick recap: Bathsheba and the king of Israel, David, had an affair while her husband was away at war. Bathsheba got pregnant, and to cover it up, David had her husband killed in battle. David then took Bathsheba as his own (seventh) wife.

Pretty scandalous. About as dirty as it gets, huh? One would think God never could bless a woman, or a marriage, after something like that. But God's grace is infinitely bigger than *any* of our mistakes.

In River's book, David and Bathsheba both fully and wholly

repent of their sins once they are convicted of what they have done. Even though they lose their first son conceived in the affair, Bathsheba goes on to become David's favorite wife, who bears him four sons.

In fact, it was her son Solomon, not all the other sons before him from the other wives, who became heir to David's throne and was entrusted with God's people.

Who would have ever seen *that* coming? But that's the kind of love God has for us.

"Your God still loves you. His plan has not been erased because of your mistake. In this crossroad, run toward His open arms and begin anew." —Suzanne Eller, Author and Speaker

Sit Down and Shut Up

The year 2013 was a big one in my life. God showed up in some extraordinary ways.

In hindsight, I can see how God was laying the groundwork way before His Big Show that year.

The first time I heard Jennifer Beckham speak was in April of 2011. She did a talk called "Whoever Asked You to Feel?" based on one of the lessons from her book *Get Over Yourself*. My interest in her was stirred, and I read her book after that conference. I found her words encouraging and insightful, and I was anxious to hear more from her.

But it was during the next two times I heard her speak that I felt as if God was speaking directly to me through her. The transparency and vulnerability with which she told her story and delivered her messages gave me a glimpse of a way I might be able to be used by God, *despite* what I had been through and the things I had done.

In the meantime, I connected with her on Facebook and we traded a few messages. She had even purchased a copy of the children's book I wrote and published around that time.

In September 2012, during her talk "Try or Train," I heard

her say that over the years some well-meaning church people had told her to stop talking about her past, as if she were dwelling on it. It made her question herself and her message. Were they right? Should she stop telling her story and only preach "happy thoughts"? And that's when she heard God clearly instruct her, *As long as your story keeps leading them to My story, keep telling it.* She realized that by sharing all her ugly and her pain and her struggle, people could feel like they were not alone and didn't need to feel pressure to be perfect for God to use them in powerful ways.

During that talk she also confessed she has to battle the voices of shame in her head daily.

"The first voice of shame," Jennifer explained, "tells you, 'You're not good enough, you're not pretty enough, you're not smart enough, you're not *enough*.' And once you've overcome that one, the second voice of shame [which was definitely the one I was hearing loud and clear at the time] comes in right behind it and says, 'Sit down and shut up because no one wants to hear what you have to say anyway. Who do you think you are?'"

> "You must learn to hush the demons that whisper, 'No one wants to read this. This has already been said. Your voice doesn't matter.' In the rare moments when the voices finally hush, you might hear the angels sing."
>
> -Margaret Feinberg

I will add that I was also hearing, "What do you have to say that someone else hasn't already said before? What can you teach that someone much more qualified than you couldn't? Does what you have to say even really matter? Who would listen to you?"

I even went through a period of time shortly after I started writing this book that I refused to read any more books for fear that I would read something too close to what I was writing and decide, "What's the point?"

This very week I cracked open a new book by Andy Stanley

and saw the first chapter was titled "The Right Person Myth."[36] *You've got to be kidding me?* was my first thought. That sounds an awful lot like "The Myth of Prince Charming," right? Then I flipped to the first page and read the words he had written to his publisher: "Although I insisted all this had been said before, you convinced me it needed to be said *again*." Thanks for that one, Andy.

A New Vision

At the beginning of 2013, God gave me the very clear vision that I was going to write books and speak on stage with Jennifer Beckham.

Although I had been a writer all my life, I had never written anything but fiction, editorials, and poetry. I had no idea how to write anything to help someone else. Nor did I have any idea what I would even teach someone if I tried! But God reminded me, *As long as your story keeps leading them to My story, keep telling it.* I realized I was supposed to tell my story, but what lessons did I have to share? What did *I* have to teach people?

The Woman at the Well

In April of 2013, while speaking at a conference I was attending, Jennifer asked me to come on stage to help with her illustration. (Understand at this time, I was nothing more than a fan of hers and a casual connection on Facebook.) During her talk, I was the "Woman at the Well" from the book of John (4:4–42). "Zacchaeus" and "Peter" both sat on stage with me as she taught another lesson about the shame we wear. She pulled black plastic garbage bags down over each of us as she spoke and symbolically ripped them off at the end.

Jennifer had no idea how ironic the entire situation was at the time. I was living with my then-boyfriend, so I had more in common with that woman at the well than she could have imagined.

It wasn't until after the event when I was looking at the pictures, thinking, *I was on stage with Jennifer Beckham!* that God reminded me He had already told me it would happen. In the weeks following that event, I found out Jennifer was working on her second book, and I remembered God's other vision for me.

Building Blocks

In May 2013, Barry and I got engaged.

Part of the requirements for our premarital "Building Blocks" course at our church was writing out our spiritual journey statement. These statements were designed to help couples communicate with each other about their individual spiritual journeys, because what you believe spiritually is foundational to a marriage. The letters provided an opportunity for us to learn more about each other, how we've grown, and our desires for growth after our wedding.

Barry's was a page and a half (I'm sure that's typical). Mine was thirteen pages. For the first time in my life, I started to get a picture of my story, my testimony.

Having grown up in church, I had heard that word thrown around, and had even heard other people share their testimonies. But I never really knew what my testimony was, or if I even had one.

My spiritual fallout and reconstruction after my divorce had been the first time in my life I had truly experienced an intimate, personal interaction with God, as embarrassing as that is to admit. For the first time, I felt like I *needed* saving. I wasn't that perfect girl anymore. I wasn't doing everything I "should be" doing. I was dirty, damaged, and worth discarding.

I was drowning in a sea of negativity and worthlessness. I was running full speed and grasping at anything I could get my hands on to find some solid ground, some satisfaction. But everything was quicksand and I was sinking fast. And then I was gloriously rescued by Him. He chose me anyway. When I had nothing good or clean or pure or whole left to offer, He still wanted me. He still pursued me. He still loved me. And once you experience what that feels like, you can't ever un-feel it.

Have you experienced this feeling? The overwhelming sense of receiving a gift you know you don't deserve? It will literally change your life when you do. You feel humbled and grateful, and all you want to do is share it with other people.

By writing my entire journey down, I began to see how my story could touch and affect others who were experiencing the same things. I realized how much the stories of divorce and remarriage that I had read had helped me through the same process, and now I could do for others what so many had done for me. Pay it forward.

A clear picture started forming in my mind. *This is my testimony*, I thought while staring at those pages. *This is the story I'm supposed to tell.*

But I didn't have any idea how much of the story there still was to be written! God was still showing up and showing off.

I WANT TO INSPIRE PEOPLE. I WANT SOMEONE TO LOOK AT ME AND SAY, "BECAUSE OF YOU I DIDN'T GIVE UP".
- Unknown

Nice to Meet You. Want to Get Married?

In August of that year, Jennifer Beckham and I made a date to have brunch. It was the first time we would be talking more than just in passing at a conference, and I was unbelievably nervous.

The night before I told my husband I was worried about freaking her out. "Barry, it's not like I can just show up and say, 'Hi! You're my hero. I know you don't know me that well, but God told me we're going to write a book together.' That would be like the guy on the first date who tells the chick he's going to marry her. Creeper. I can't be a creeper."

When we sat down, I wanted to pick her brain about writing. She gave me some great tips. I told her my story and how I felt God had spoken to me through her messages and that I was being called to share my experiences. I told her I had an outline prepared, and she asked me if she could read it. I sheepishly slid her a copy of my thirteen-page spiritual journey statement I brought with me in the hopes she would be willing to do just that.

More than anything, I was seeking validation that day. I needed her to read my words and tell me, "Yes, there is a place for this story; it needs to be heard." I needed to know I had something worth saying.

This $#!t Just Got Real

You know how people begin reminiscing about major world events by saying, "I'll never forget where I was or what I was doing when . . ."? Well, I can tell you I was standing in my hotel room in Times Square in New York in November 2013 when I got a text from Jennifer asking me if I could talk.

> "When you fall, make sure you pick something up while you're down there."
>
> - Jennifer Beckham

I called her right away, and she told me she had been reading my spiritual journey statement and was excited. Parts of it fit perfectly in a certain chapter she was working on in her next book. She asked if she could use my story there and even weave it throughout the book. And she asked if I would be willing to write some more things for her. Of course I responded all cool-hand-Luke with the most composure I could muster, "I would be honored for you to use my story . . . Of course you can . . . Sure, I'll put that stuff together for you."

But when I hung up the phone, I literally jumped on my hotel bed in true *Home Alone* fashion, squealing, "I'm writing a book with Jennifer Beckham! I'm *really* writing a book with Jennifer Beckham!"

It was really happening. Everything God had told me was manifesting right in front of me.

You might be wondering, *So where's that book?*

At the beginning of 2014, God threw a wrench in my plans of being a best-selling author by my thirtieth birthday (as if it was His job to follow my plans!). He called Jennifer and her husband, Anthony, to walk away from the traveling, evangelical ministry, and corporate speaking they had been doing for the last sixteen years and stay home in Jacksonville, Florida, to plant a church. Needless to say, Jen's next book got put on hold.

But God wouldn't leave me alone about telling my story. It's all I heard from Him in 2014, which happened to be the year I learned *how* to hear His voice.

Discernment and Hearing Tim's Voice

My friend Tim died suddenly in January of 2014. He was thirty-five years old. And he had one of the biggest passions for God I've ever had the privilege of seeing in action. I was with him two weeks prior, joking around, pushing, poking like the brother and sister that we weren't. Then his heart stopped beating and he was gone. I will never see him again on this earth.

After his death, I was struggling with the decision of whether to attend his funeral or a Christian leadership conference that was coming up the same weekend. My husband and I were going to be taking a friend with us to the conference who had tried to commit suicide two weeks before, so we felt it was really important that we both be there with him the entire time.

As I contemplated the decision, I struggled with the worry of either being judged by people for not going to the funeral, considering I claimed to be such good friends with Tim, or disappointing others if I decided to go and missed part of the conference. Scriptures like Luke 9:60, "Let the dead bury the dead . . ." echoed in mind.

While battling with what I should do, I heard Tim say as clear as a bell in my head, "Rach, of course you need to go the conference. Don't worry about me."

And that was that. My decision was made. Other people's opinion's aside, I knew what I needed to do.

Because I *knew* Tim, I knew his heart. I knew his passion and his calling in life. Because I had touched him, heard his voice, and saw his face; because I knew the inflection he used when he spoke, the shape his mouth made when it formed words, and the expressions his eyes gave when he told a story, I knew what he would want me to do in that situation.

And then it dawned on me—that's how well I need to know and recognize God's voice. I wanted it to be that clear and unquestioning. I never wanted to doubt again when I heard a directive if it was from God or my own head.

I began to wonder, *What do I need to do to recognize His voice that clearly?* The answer was by getting to know God as intimately as I knew my friend Tim. To know His heart and His desires for me, which, I learned, is always what's best for me.

It says so right in 3 John 1:2: "Beloved, I wish above ALL things that thou may prosper and be in health, even as thy soul prospers."

As I pondered all of this, for the first time in my life the idea of discernment clicked for me. I made a revelation I can never unmake. Really, truly being able to hear from and follow God's voice became a little more believable for me, and I had a clear mission and plan on how to get to that place.

Even after he left the earth, my friend Tim was still teaching me new things.

Now that I've learned how to hear God's voice, I'm working on obedience—every time, not just when I like it. It's a process. And I'm still not perfect, nor will I ever be in this life.

Healed People Heal People

We've all heard the expression "hurting people hurt people," but the other half of that is also true: "Healed people heal people."

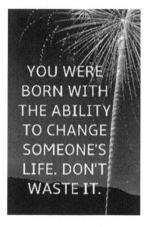

Throughout 2013 and 2014, God continually brought divorced people and people considering divorce into my life. For the first time, I was able to empathize with their pain and have compassion for them because I had already been through that pain myself.

Prior to going through my divorce, I was extremely judgmental. When I met other divorced or divorcing people, I gave them the standard, "Oh gosh, well, at least you didn't have kids" response (which is not helpful, by the way, I now know) and then walked away thinking about all the things they probably didn't do to meet their spouses needs that caused their divorce.

But now my heart only breaks for them. I want to tell them they are not alone. I want to tell them it does get better, and one day it will stop hurting. And I want to tell them they will have dreams again.

During that time, two marriages were saved in part because they had taken the advice I was able to give them. And others were at least comforted by someone who could listen and understand, who could recommend books that would help begin the healing process.

I was starting to see the real-life application of how my divorce could be used for good and to believe that it had not been in vain. I could see now I was able to really help other people, not just preach at them from a place of merciless indifference. I could save marriages and help heal wounded hearts from divorce.

That would be enough, but God wasn't finished with me yet. Remember above and beyond what we can think or imagine? There was more He was going to show me about this new vision.

Bigger Than Divorce

In chapter 4, I talked about my first vision being to work with and speak to teenage girls. One part of that dream had always been to go back and work as a counselor at the church camp I attended growing up.

After my divorce, I imagined that was out of the question. All sorts of thoughts ran through my mind: *Why would they want someone as tainted as I am to be an influence in these young girls' lives? What would they think of me? Should I hide that I*

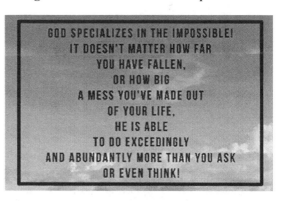

GOD SPECIALIZES IN THE IMPOSSIBLE!
IT DOESN'T MATTER HOW FAR
YOU HAVE FALLEN,
OR HOW BIG
A MESS YOU'VE MADE OUT
OF YOUR LIFE,
HE IS ABLE
TO DO EXCEEDINGLY
AND ABUNDANTLY MORE THAN YOU ASK
OR EVEN THINK!

have been divorced? What if they found out? Surely they know plenty of people from my parents' church who know me, but what do those people think of me now? Would they want me working with their kids?

Then came the self-righteous thoughts that were just as bad: *Well, if they are going to judge me and not let God use me in those*

*girls' lives, then that's on them. That's their own sin, and they'll
have to answer for it.*

God still has to remind me today not to be so disgusted by
religious "church people." The legalists. The denomination-ists.
The ones who don't "get it." Those who are more eager to assign
scarlet letters to individuals with sordid pasts rather than
welcome them with open arms.

I had an extreme prejudice against these religious people for
a while; *you know, after I stopped being one of them myself.* But
God has shown me their sin is just different from my sin. If I can
love on and extend grace to someone like me, those who have
had an affair or are going through a divorce, then surely I can
love on and extend grace to my brothers and sisters in the body
of Christ, even if we didn't see eye to eye on some things.

I still remember the knots in my stomach as I fired off an e-
mail to the new camp director asking him if they needed
volunteers for that summer. I spent several anxious days
waiting for his reply, and was elated when my offer was
accepted.

Just walking onto the camp grounds the first day of the
faculty prep meeting was a victory for me. I had been accepted,
affirmed, validated, allowed to serve. I knew I didn't *need* their
stamp of approval because I already had one from God, but I still
wanted it. Is that something I need to work on? Probably.

It was also a validation *of them* to me. God was showing me
these "church people" weren't as judgmental as I thought.

I was overjoyed for the opportunity to make a mark, no
matter how small, in those students' lives. To be given even the
slightest bit of influence in their minds and hearts, in their
futures, was a dream come true. What a shame it would have
been if I hadn't sent that e-mail? If I had let all my fearful
questions and pessimistic thoughts talk me out of trying. I never
would have experienced all that I did that week.

Amazing things happened during those six days that

summer. But one serendipitous miracle that occurred the last night stands out.

I walked back in the dorm to find one of the girls crying while talking with one of the other counselors in the bathroom.

"Hey, girl! Everything okay?" I asked, sliding an arm around her shoulders.

The beautiful young blonde smiled weakly and shook her head. "No. Not really." When I asked her to explain, she said, "I'm just sick to my stomach thinking about camp ending and going back home tomorrow to my negative environment. When I'm here, it's so easy to be myself. But back at my home and my school, I have to pretend to be something I'm not just to fit in."

She went on to tell me stories of her high school experience. She told me about her friend who had committed suicide the year prior and was still being made fun of, even though he was gone. She told me they even mocked her while she was crying, mourning his loss.

"Girl, I can't even begin to imagine what you're going through. High school was nothing like that when I was there. Sure, there was bullying, but it's at a whole different level today." I paused. "One thing I have learned is that when people hurt me, when they are mean to me or they say or do things I don't understand, I have learned to stop thinking about myself and shift my focus for a minute to think about what is going on in their lives. Something must be causing them to hurt this badly that they would do and say these things to me. It's not about you, really. And as soon as you realize that, you stop being hurt yourself and your heart breaks for that person. It takes your eyes off you, and when you look at the bigger picture, you can no longer be offended."

As we talked, other girls filed into the bathroom and joined the conversation.

One girl shared that her dad had left their family and gotten remarried, and that her mom worked two jobs to support them. She had to come home from school every day and play substitute mother to her three-year-old sister. She felt like she had lost her childhood because of it.

Another talked about her parents getting divorced and how she felt so alone because none of her other friends had divorced parents, so she didn't have anyone to talk to about it.

With each new story—about their lives, their schools, their peers, their families—I don't even know how to describe the shock I experienced. These were the "good Christian kids," from "Christian" homes! My naïveté told me that these type of things are only supposed to happen to all those *other people* out there! I was overwhelmed, and my heart broke for each of them.

As I struggled to wrap my mind around everything they shared, I told them, "Here's what I can tell you, more than anything else right now, your number one priority and focus has *got* to be controlling your mind, protecting it. You've got to dilute all the negative that's streaming into your minds and your hearts every day with as much positive as humanly possible. You have to, or you're not going to be able to keep your head above water, you're just going to drown in all that negative."

Then, for whatever reason, I told them my story. I told them about how when I went through my divorce I was broken and hurting and how I bottomed out. I shared all the horrible lies that were going through my mind that I wrote in my journal that one night. I told them I ran from God and how He passionately pursued me. I told them about the books I read and the things I learned.

They asked me to make a recommended reading list for them and I did. I also gave them suggestions for uplifting and empowering audio recordings of Jennifer Beckham, Joyce

Meyer, and Lisa Bevere.

At the end of our conversation, one of the girls said, "Thank you for telling us your story. Out of the whole week of camp, literally, everything you just said in the last ten minutes is exactly what I needed to hear. This is what I came to camp for."

And then it hit me. In that moment, I realized the impossible truth that my story can help more than just the mid-twenties divorcée. It can help sixteen- and seventeen-year-old girls going through completely different things than I ever experienced. And probably many others.

I saw God smiling down as I had that revelation and laughed back at Him, saying, "Okay, I get it, just keep telling it."

You

So it's you. Yes, you, dear, sweet reader, are exactly the reason I have written this book.

You are not the reason for the failure of my marriage. God did

not *make* that happen as a "test" or a "lesson" for me; that was a result of a series of my own bad decisions. But you are the reason I can be completely redeemed from it and know that I have a purpose, that I can still be used by God.

Thank you for that. Thank you for giving me the opportunity to speak life and hope into your heart and spirit.

Now, Tell Your Story

Are you starting to see how other people might be able to benefit from your "Now What?" moment? Maybe you're not there yet, maybe it's still too fresh, and that's okay. You'll get there. Just keep your eyes open. I promise there is a way God will be able to use your story for your good. He will not let your pain be pointless.

Paul even said it himself in Romans 8:28: "And we know that in *all things* God works for the good of those who love him, who have been called according to His purpose." All things includes the really suck things. The things we get ourselves into *and* the things that are out of our control, or that other people do to us. All things.

what if I fall?
oh, but my darling,
what if you *fly?*
- R.H.

At the end of this book I've included a "'Now What?' Questionnaire" for you to use to walk through telling your story. Even if it's just to yourself right now. The questions will help you see the turning points and possibilities. You may even learn things you haven't realized yet about what you've gone through.

I know several of the people I interviewed for the stories in Part 2 experienced new revelations as we worked through it. Hopefully reading them will help you bring that picture a little more into focus by hearing different people's perspectives.

You have a story. As long as it keeps leading people to God's story, keep telling it.

Recommended Books for

Chapter Nine

- *Get Over Yourself: 7 Principles to Get Over Your Past and on with Your Purpose* by Jennifer Beckham
- *Outwitting the Devil* by Napoleon Hill
- *I Thought It Was Just Me (But It Isn't)* by Brené Brown
  Brené Brown is the world's leading authority on shame and vulnerability. She has done extensive research and written multiple books exploring the subject.
- *Life Without Limits* by Nick Vujicic
  Born without arms or legs, Nick Vujicic overcame his disability to live not just independently but a rich, fulfilling life, becoming a model for anyone seeking true happiness.

Chapter Ten

"Dare to write a fresh chapter."

- Unknown

So, What's Next?

"It's easy to come up with a reason why we can't be happy, why we can't accomplish a dream, why we can't overcome a problem. As long as you're making excuses you'll justify staying where you are. Don't use excuses as permission to settle for less than God's best."
—*Joel Osteen*

Forewarning: Depending on where you are in your journey, this may be a chapter you have to come back to at a later time. I know when I was in the middle of my "moment," just getting up and remembering to eat that day was a tally mark in the win column.

If you've just experienced your life-altering circumstance I call your "Now What?" moment, you probably aren't ready to start making new plans for your future yet. You probably can't see past the pain you're feeling and into a new vision for your life. You may still be grieving over the loss of your first dream. And that's okay. Grief is not an overnight process, nor is it something you will likely get through by the end of this book. But I want you to know there is more out there for you. Your life, your purpose, is not over.

Read this chapter now, and if you aren't quite ready for it, put it on the shelf and come back for it later. Just make sure you come back for it. The world is waiting on you.

I'm sure by now you're thinking, *This all sounds great, Rachel. I'm happy you've been able to come full circle, but how do I figure out what* my *purpose is in life?*

First of all, there are a lot of people more qualified and better at articulating this topic than I am. (I've included an awesome list of books to start with at the end of this chapter.) One of them is Rick Warren's short book called *What on Earth Am I Here For?* It's an excerpt from his more widely known *Purpose Driven Life* material. This little booklet is the most thought-provoking and potentially life-altering fifty-nine pages you'll ever read.

I recommend you at least get to thinking about your purpose. I do know this much: it will be bigger than you, and it will involve touching other people's lives.

I don't believe we will ever be truly satisfied in any

 relationship, any job, any home, any car, any city, or any church even, if we aren't actively pursuing the purpose God put us on this earth to walk out.

Do you know that you were created for a purpose?

Do you know that you were uniquely designed to fill a specific purpose in God's bigger picture and plan for this earth?

Have you ever thought about that before?

A good place to start thinking about it is by making a list of things you're passionate about. Go ahead. Do it right now. This is not a list of things you like, are mildly interested in, or do as a hobby, but things that make your heart race faster or bring tears to your eyes when they come to mind. Things that call out to the deepest parts of your soul and beg you to be involved in or support.

On my list are things like pleasing God with my life, adoption, freedom (in every form), eradicating abortion, and restoring American exceptionalism.

Things I'm Passionate About:

_____

_____

_____

_____

_____

Next make a list of the things you're good at—your natural talents and abilities, or skills you've developed in your life.

Things I'm Good At:

_____

_____

_____

_____

_____

Now look at those two lists together. How do you think you could use the things you are good at to be involved with or further the mission of the things you're passionate about?

Do you see a correlation yet?

Finally, think about your experiences in life, your "Now What?" moments. This is the real game-changer. All those things you thought were derailing you in life, your failures, setbacks, detours, were actually preparing you. Flunking out of college, the broken marriage, that job you

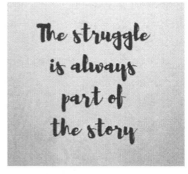
The struggle is always part of the story

lost, the business that failed, the accident you were in, that injury, that loss, that miscarriage or abortion, the abuse . . . You can use what you have gone through to help other people. To touch others' lives. To build hope, spark inspiration, or just relate and let someone know they are not alone.

My friend Leslie was hit by a drunk driver, and she still lives with remnants of glass in her face and legs and walks with a severe limp. She speaks to groups of people about the dangers and real-life consequences of drinking and driving to raise awareness and hopefully prevent what happened to her from happening to other people.

That seems like such an obvious correlation now, but it wasn't so obvious when she was lying in a hospital bed wondering if she was going to live. Or when she was riding around in a wheelchair for over a year wondering if she would ever walk again, crying, "Why me, God? I wasn't the one drinking or being irresponsible." But today she is changing people's lives for the better and literally saving others.

I promise, if you sit in a quiet place and meditate on those lists, if you ask God to open your eyes, speak to your heart, and give you clarity, wisdom, and understanding, you will start to see your purpose forming in your mind.

I believe God created you with these unique talents and abilities *on purpose*. And I believe He planted those deepest desires in your heart for a reason.

Once I made those lists it became really easy to say no to the things that weren't on them—the things I was mildly interested in or felt obligated to be a part of. I

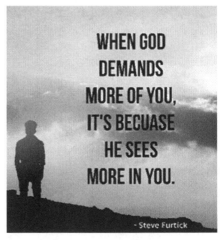

WHEN GOD DEMANDS MORE OF YOU, IT'S BECUASE HE SEES MORE IN YOU.

- Steve Furtick

could let all that go and not feel guilty. This exercise gave me clarity and focus. It became much easier to make decisions about where to invest my time, my talents, and my finances. I could start filtering every decision through: *Will this get me closer to or take me further away from my purpose?*

Have you ever struggled with a decision, wondering, *Is this what God really wants me to do? Should I go here? Do this? Buy that? Invest in this cause or business? Date that person?*

Once you clearly identify the things on your lists, it becomes much easier to determine what you're supposed to do with your life.

And the next terrifying step is: Go do it.

Seriously.

Go.

Deuteronomy 1:21 says, "See, the LORD your God has set the land before you. Go up and take possession of it as Yahweh, the God of your fathers, has told you. Do not be afraid or discouraged."

This verse and the following reflection recently hit my inbox in "The Daily" devotional e-mail I receive from my church:

When God gives us the go-ahead to move, it's time to go. Period. Fear is already planning to make a run at you. Discouragement or hopelessness may follow behind. Try not to give them the time-of-day. Expect them. And keep moving. God may show us something awesome and tell us to "go get it." Character and faith will be formed as we move. If we want the good stuff, God may well have it for us, but it's pretty typical of God to invite us to move, fight, go, as he clears the way. We're going to have to get off our "you-know-what" and fight a bit to take it.[37]

If you aren't currently in a positon in life that allows you to move toward your purpose, change it. If your job is holding you back, get a different job. If you need more money, go make it or raise it. If your circle of friends or acquaintances are a hindrance or distraction right now, distance yourself from them and make new friends.

(Note: If you're married and your spouse is not on board

with your vision, this is *not* permission to leave your spouse and go find a new one. Start working on your vision and pray they decide to come along. Once they see you are serious, I bet they will, at the very least, be supportive. But I don't believe God would call you to do something that would cause your marriage to fail, so if it is, maybe that's not what He called you to do. Or you've got to find a way to make it work and still show your spouse they are a priority as well. It's not easy, but it will be worth it.)

The founders of {well} studio and authors of *Thirty-One Days of Prayer for the Dreamer and the Doer* call this command for action "the burden of a dream."

The sooner you identify what your dream/calling/purpose is and start moving in that direction, the fuller and more satisfying your *whole* life—your work, your relationships, your downtime—will be. I promise.

I also assure you as soon as you start moving in that direction, you will meet resistance. Because, like we talked about earlier, you have an enemy. You and God have the same enemy, actually, and the last thing that guy wants to see is you fulfilling the purpose for which God created you. He has no interest in you positively impacting other people, this world, or God's kingdom. I'm telling you this now, not to scare you, but so you can be prepared.

Your enemy is clever and a master at deception. He wants to steal your dream, to scare you with unknowns, to paralyze you with the fear of what-if's, to distract you, maybe even with things that look "good" on the outside. He will remind you of your past failures to discourage you. He wants nothing more than for you to give up and decide it's just not worth it, to determine that your dream is just too hard or would take too long to accomplish. He would love to keep you right in the middle of your comfort zone, where it's safe and you never even try to do anything remarkable with your life. After all, he'll try to convince you, your life isn't *so* bad. You do *some* good things.

I once heard someone say, "There is a good, acceptable, and perfect will for your life, and you get to choose which one you receive." Don't settle. Don't give up God's perfect plan for a counterfeit or anything less. Don't compromise. Don't give in to the fear tactics of your enemy. Keep moving. You were created for great things. Now.

This doesn't mean life will be perfect, that you will not have more letdowns in the future. It's easy to build up a fantasy of how life should go and become disenchanted when that doesn't turn out exactly as you imagined. But I believe we should never stop reaching toward what God is calling us.

> What's the point of being alive if you don't at least try to do something remarkable? How very odd, to believe God gave you life, and yet not think that life asks more of you than watching TV...
>
> – John Green

I recently heard pastor and author Steve Furtick say, "What if reaching *is* the goal? What if the thing God wanted from me all along was not that I would arrive, but that I would reach? What if what He really wants from you, what if the real goal is just that you keep reaching?"

I'm sure we've all seen the inspirational poster with the similar sentiment: "Success is in the journey, not the destination." It's universally true. And I think part of that reaching is reaching more people. There are always more people you and your story can impact.

Philippians 2:13 promises, "For it is God who works in you to will and to act in order to fulfill His good purposes."

Yeah, but I've Already Tried That

What if you already know your purpose and were already moving toward it when your "Now What?" moment hit? Or you've drifted away from it for some other reason? Life has beaten you down. You have already experienced those attacks of the enemy and it just got too hard. You are not alone.

I have always had vision boards up in my bedroom. I was probably sixteen when I pasted together and hung my first one. I've moved them to every apartment and house I have ever lived in (and I've moved a lot!). I hung them when I was first on my own, living in a low-income apartment. I would often only have ten dollars left over at the end of the week for groceries and looking at the boards inspired me to keep dreaming. At all times I saw the pictures of the types of houses I wanted to live in, the cars I wanted to drive, the places I wanted to see, and the intangible things— 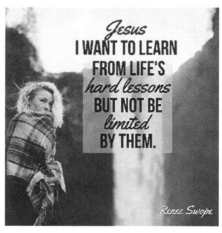 children to adopt, relationships I would have, the impact I would make. And I was reminded that where I was, was not where I was staying. My circum-stances and surroundings were only temporary as long as I kept moving forward.

The first place I lived after my divorce, I didn't hang my vision boards up. I felt so far removed from those pictures, from ever seeing those dreams come to fruition. I just couldn't see how that life was possible anymore.

When Barry and I moved into our first house together, I pulled them all out and cried. I still wasn't sure I believed in them, but I was more disheartened that I had given up on dreaming all together.

When I shared this with Barry, he went out and bought fresh poster board and insisted we make new ones together.

Even though my old ones still had some things on them I liked, they were from a totally different place in my life. I took a couple things from them, but I wanted a new vision board to match the new vision in my life. That's the power of vision boards. When you constantly have the images of what you want your life to look like in front of your eyes, your imagination and subconscious mind go to work to make those things manifest in the physical realm. They will find a way, attracting ideas and people and opportunities to you.

While creating my new vision board, I found this one small quote I cut out of a magazine that meant the most to me. I don't even remember what it was in reference to, but it said, "Your dreams miss you." I get emotional just typing that now. Those four words were such a simple, sweet reminder to me that I was called and created for more than the complacency I was settling for.

I had dreams inside me just waiting to get out, but I had allowed myself to move far away from them. I had forgotten them, left them behind. I'd buried them in my day-to-day routine and busyness to keep my mind off what I had been through and the fact that I was stagnant in life.

My dreams missed me.

And I missed them.

Your dreams miss you.

I give you permission to dream again.

A Parting Battle Cry

I recently heard Pastor Gary Newell give this rallying speech on a leadership development CD and it gets my blood pumping every time:

> "It's hard changing your life, but it's worth it. Some of you haven't accomplished what you thought you would have by now because of your *feelings*. Every day you say no to your dreams, you are pushing those dreams back by months, maybe even years. That one 'you didn't *feel* like it' day can push your dreams back. Don't allow your

emotions to control you. If you don't discipline your feelings, they will use you.

Have you gotten comfortable? Have you been compromising? Are you procrastinating? Are you challenging yourself? Is your life an adventure or boring?

Surround yourself with people who are hungry, people who are unstoppable, people who refuse to quit, people who want more. Attach yourself to winners. Invest in yourself. Get excited about doing a great work. About being your best you. You are an uncommon breed. You can touch thousands of lives. You are a special miracle. You can always, always better your best. Decide to push yourself. Be resilient. Be restless. Easy is not an option.

The next chapter of your life hasn't been written yet and it matters how you finish. Live on purpose and scream to the world, 'It's not over till I win!'"[38]

Recommended Books for

Chapter Ten

- *What on Earth Am I Here For?* by Rick Warren
- *Thirty-One Days of Prayer for the Dreamer and the Doer* by Jenn Sprinkle and Kelly Rucker
- *Restless: Because You Were Made for More* by Jennie Allen
- *Imagine Big* by Terri Savelle Foy
  Terri has also produced a wonderful dream journal to go along with this book. She walks you through imagining your life five years from now. I loved putting mine together, and I revisit the pages and pictures often!
- *The Dream Giver* by Bruce Wilkinson
  A modern-day parable about Ordinary, who dares to leave the Land of Familiar to pursue his Big Dream. With the help of the Dream Giver, he battles the enemy called Average. Wilkinson gives readers practical, biblical keys to fulfilling their own dream, revealing that there's no limit to what God can accomplish when we choose to pursue the dreams He gives us for His honor.
- *The Magic of Thinking Big* by David J Schwartz
  One of the top-selling and widely read self-development books of all time.
- *The Pursuit: Success Is Hidden in the Journey* by Dexter Yager
- *Live the Dream: No More Excuses* by Larry Winters
- *Make It Happen* by Lara Casey
- *Undaunted: Daring to Do What God Calls You to Do* by Christine Caine

"As long as you have breath, your story is still being written. You may be in a difficult scene right now, but you have to remind yourself, that's not how your story ends. You have an expected end. The Creator of the universe, the Most High God has already planned it for good and not harm."

—Joel Osteen

Part Two

Other People's
"Now What?" Moments

Chapter Eleven

"I know people who feel like they've wasted
years of their lives because of poor choices.
They spent years in a relationship that was toxic, years
with an addiction, years at a job where
they weren't fulfilled. But you have to realize,
nothing you've been through is ever wasted.
Your past experiences, good and bad,
have deposited something on the inside of you.
Those challenges have sharpened you,
to make you who you are today."

- Unknown

Running Doesn't Work

"Owning our story can be hard, but not nearly as difficult as spending our lives running from it."
—Brené Brown

Now you know my story, but what if you're story is completely different than mine? Can my lessons still apply to you? Will God really meet you where you are? And if He did, what would that even look like?

To answer these questions, I'd like to share a few other people's stories with you. People whose "Now What?" moments are completely different from mine, from jail to rejection to medical diagnosis. But the bottom line is still the same:

"God's plan for your life is bigger than everything coming against it."
—Kenneth Copeland

When God gave me the idea to tell other people's stories in this book, a few people came to mind right away. People I had personally witnessed going through their own "Now What?" moments who came out stronger and more beautiful on the other side.

The challenging part, though, has been finding more people who have truly turned their moment over to God and are letting Him fully redeem and restore their story.

There are countless people who have had life-altering "Now What?" moments but are still sitting in the fallout of it. They are stagnant in their anger and bitterness. Replaying their grievances over and over. Feeling justified in holding on to those negative emotions. They are still playing the role of victim.

I am watching some people right now who are running full speed in *any* direction they think will take them away from that place. They are throwing themselves into other relationships, jobs, or projects, even moving across the country. They will do *anything* to keep themselves busy so they don't have to stop and think about or deal with the mess on the inside. They've locked it up in a box and thrown it into the deepest part of the ocean of their soul. The only problem is, no matter where you go, there you are. No matter who you're with, *you* are with them.

Can I tell you something? Running doesn't work. Just coping doesn't work. Relying on another crutch without dealing with the brokenness doesn't work. Period.

Think about your life as a garden or a field. You can go out into that field every day, rain or shine, hot or cold, and chop down the weeds shooting up in your crop. You will always have plenty of work to do because until you deal with the *root* of those weeds, they are just going to keep creeping back up above ground. And choking out the roots of the good stuff you've planted under the surface.

Do you know what I'm talking about? Have you tried dealing with things by *not* dealing with them? Just not bringing them up again or thinking about them? How effective has that been in the past?

Take Maria, for example, whose husband, Chuck, confessed his pornography addiction four months before their wedding. Chuck sought restoration and accountability right away and has fully overcome his addiction. But Maria ran from the bitterness, anger, and resentment, the disappointment and disgust that rooted itself inside her that day for six years. Their intimacy and their marriage suffered. And she could keep telling herself it was *his* fault for the rest of her life while remaining in that hollow pit herself.

Chuck was walking around completely free; a renewed man, fully abiding in God's grace. But Maria's spirit was shriveling up and rotting more and more each day.

It wasn't until she stopped denying her brokenness, acknowledged her baggage from Chuck's past, and sought healing that God could start restoring her from the inside out.

She recently spoke about what that journey looked like from stage at our church:

> "I am not what happened to me, I am what I choose to become."
> - Carl Gustav Jung

When I found out about his addiction, we were driving from Pennsylvania to Cincinnati. We were in the car and I was driving. He told me he needed to tell me something. [After he did,] it became quiet in the car, and I felt rage.

The first thing I did was put up the music and I slammed on the gas; we were going about 120 miles an hour. And the way it works in Pennsylvania is you go on round-abouts, and there are cliffs as you go around them. I literally contemplated going over one. In that moment, I hated him. I didn't think about the future, I didn't think about our wedding, I didn't think about anything.

I wish there was a stronger word than anger. I don't know if enraged is it, but that's what I felt. It was like the Tasmanian devil inside churning, and I was unable to release that. That's how it felt.

But along with that, it felt shameful, shameful at the idea that that's what he did. And I did think for a moment, *what is it that I have not done, that he needed to go that route?* I almost blamed myself.

I figuratively created a little box, and I put that information in a box, and I stuffed it inside my gut. A callous formed around that and I never talked to him about it again. I never talked to anyone about it again. Because it was a private issue. Ya know, I was told growing up, anything behind closed doors, stays behind closed doors. So I had no tools. No way of sharing what I felt—my feelings, my emotions to him—I didn't know how to describe them or label them. So I stuffed them away.

He began to get help. He began to get counseling, accountability partners, he started a recovery group. . . . And I "forgot" about it.

But it manifested itself in our relationship in that I didn't trust him. I became very angry, very quickly. Anytime we were watching a movie that would show a woman, I would think, *Oh, he's thinking about her, he's fantasizing about her.* But I never said to him exactly what I was feeling, I just became angry. Our intimacy suffered tremendously.

When I enrolled in "Deliverance from Strongholds," I think that's when I even touched on the subject for the first time. God was like said, "Maria, I'm going to put free women in front of you, and I just want you to share your heart, and I will be there to protect you." And I did! And it was freeing!

I released all the *gooky* stuff, but the box was still there; so the callous was coming off, but the box was still there and that's when for me I think, I realized, I need professional counseling. And Chuck was overjoyed! He was elated! He was like, "Let's go! I'll make the appointment. Let's go."

Once we started counseling, I felt like the therapist was on my side and someone wanted to hear my story. Not just Chuck's story, 'cause he had told it over and over. And he had received help. It was at that point, where I felt open and vulnerable enough to share my story, and the therapist was a safe person.

And today, God is equipping me with the strength to be able to talk about it, to be able to share with thousands.

You know if you would have asked me to do this [stand on stage and tell my story] five years ago, I would have been like, "HELLLL NO!" But there's such a freedom in it!

There's a . . . I want to say Joy, but it's bigger, it's bigger than that. It's like a hallelujah!

And the gates have opened. But it's not water rushing in— it's sun! After a rainstorm, where the clouds have rolled a way, the thunder - you can hear it in the distance—it's gone. And the sun, you can feel it. That's where we are . . . [Her voice cracks as she finishes.] Yeah, we're basking in that sun.

Sometimes God moves our mountains and sometimes God says, "Take another lap".

Let me assure you, everything does not have to be perfect before you can experience that same sunlight. Let go, stop trying and stop working, and let those broken places be healed.

It could—but likely won't—happen overnight. But it *does* take a decision on your part to take that first step—courageously, shakingly, uncertainly—in that right direction. It's messy and never looks the same for two people. But you just keep moving that direction one step, one day, at a time. Relentlessly.

You will have days of setbacks, when you relapse in your anger, or hurt, or disappointment. And that's okay. There will be days when you can't see it all coming together. But it is, dear one.

Sometimes God takes you the long route to your place of deliverance because there are things He is looking to develop in you that you'll be able to use once you get to your Promised Land. Just look at the Israelites' story. God had them wandering in the desert for forty years because they couldn't get over themselves. Their mind-set, their attitude, was all wrong. And they were always focused on the wrong things. All the while, God was pruning them, teaching them to trust and rely on Him always.

Joyce Meyer has a six-part teaching series called "Wilderness Mentalities" through which she goes into great detail about the ten wrong mind-sets the Israelites had during their journey that kept them in the wilderness. "It was a three-day journey that they turned into forty years because they kept going around, and around and around the same dumb mountain!" Meyer said.

Be patient with God as He's leading you out of your wilderness, and be patient with yourself.

Be encouraged by these stories in the following pages. You are not the only one walking this path right now.

"You don't know what God can do with your broken pieces until you give God your broken pieces."
—*Nick Vujicic*

"You go nowhere by accident.

Wherever you go,

God is sending you.

Wherever you are,

God has put you there.

God has a purpose

in your being there.

Christ lives in you

and has something

he wants to do

through you where you are.

Believe this and go in the

grace and love and

power of Jesus Christ."

—Rev. Richard Halverson

Chapter Twelve

Guilty Verdict
Jessica's "Now What?" Moment

At my twenty-fifth birthday party, my friend Jessica told me about this guy she had just met. In between dances, we giggled about how cute he was as she showed me pictures on her phone. The two had met at a recent body-building competition in which they both participated. She said she really liked him. After that, I rarely saw her. Over the next year and a half, Jessica fell off the face of the planet. You know those friends, the ones who disappear into a black hole anytime they are in a relationship? Yeah, well, that wasn't really Jess, so her absence was a little concerning.

The following spring they were engaged and moving in together. I warned her about rushing into something so serious. After all, I had just made that same mistake, and it didn't end very well. Of course she did not heed my advice. In fact, she avoided me even more after that.

> EVERYTHING HAPPENS FOR A REASON. BUT SOMETIMES THE REASON IS THAT YOU'RE STUPID AND MAKE BAD DECISIONS.
> -UNKNOWN

We never want to hear the truth when we're trying so ferociously to run from it.

Almost exactly two years after that birthday party, she invited me to lunch. I was happy to hear from her and glad she had reached out. I had been worried about her, although I wasn't even remotely prepared for our conversation that day. My mouth hit the table when she told me what was going on in her life.

Turns out, Mr. Wonderful had been running a four-state-wide anabolic steroid ring that had been under investigation for two years by the DEA. Thirty-two people had been arrested, including her, and she was awaiting her trial.

Follow your heart but take your brain with you.

Right there in our booth at Applebee's she told me all the horrors she had experienced over the last two years. He was abusive and controlling; he had annihilated her verbally, emotionally, and physically. He kept her from seeing her family and friends; she wasn't allowed to leave the house without him. She knew about his "business," and he had warned her that if he was caught, he was take her down with him. He had threatened her and her family's lives and told her if she ever left he would "set her parents' house on fire."

She told me why she stayed, mostly out of fear, and also for the reasons we all do: We think we can save them. We think it's our fault they act that way, that it's our fault they treat us that way. They have convinced us we are the crazy ones, and we think if we can show them the truth, they will change. But that never works.

At the time of our lunch, she was happy that she was back home and away from him, but she was nervous about her trial. She said most of the other people involved had admitted guilt and accepted a plea bargain, but she refused to admit to something she hadn't done. She was going to tell the truth—all of it—and hoped it would set her free. She asked me to pray for her. I did, fervently. I was extremely confident they would see her duress and innocence and that all the charges would be dropped. I honestly had total peace about it.

Then the unimaginable happened. Her verdict was guilty. And with the rap of a gavel, Jessica was sentenced to five years in prison.

Today I get to see Jessica about every six weeks in a prison visitation hall with a hundred other people around.

I remember in the first months we were both angry and confused. In my letters and visits, I tried to be as positive and encouraging as possible. For the first year, all either of us could focus on or talk about was her appeal. But the day came when she got word from her lawyer that her appeal had fallen on deaf ears as well, and she was truly stuck in this place for four *more* years. Now what?

Jessica wrote the following letter to me from prison:

As far as dreams and visions for my life, I had a lot. I had achieved success in sports and in school and had every intention of going out and making a mark on the world, in one way or another. I had an amazing job, check. I was pursuing my dreams of being financially independent outside of that, check. I had a great family and great friends. I had the dream of having a family of my own, the kids and white-picket fence, and was hoping that would happen sometime soon. That my husband and I would be pursuing our goals together and helping others to do the same. The sky didn't even seem like the limit at this point.

I was developing a relationship with God for the first time in almost twenty-five years. I loved where I was and where I was going . . . until everything changed in what seems now like the blink of an eye.

God's MERCY is BIGGER than any of your mistakes.

Read Lamentations 3:22-25

Everything I had worked for, gone. The product of a brutal domestic violence relationship that had begun about two and a half years earlier. The "end" of the tangible relationship was not even good. I was separated from that man and that life because of a five-year prison sentence. Separated physically by bars, but now left to pick up the pieces, as well as continue to deal with his abuse and manipulation through mail and other means.

I went from a prisoner in my own home to a real-life prison, razor-wire and all. Every possession and dollar I had torn away. In fact, I was left with tens of thousands of debt waiting for me once I'm released. I hurt everyone in my life that means anything to me, and I had no idea who Jessica even was anymore. Alone in a crowded prison dorm I asked myself, "Now what?"

At my lowest,
God is my HOPE
At my darkest,
God is my LIGHT
At my weakeast,
God is my STRENGTH
At my saddest,
God is my COMFORTER

To be completely honest, "now what?" didn't even seem like an option. That was a stretch. Because any future at all didn't even seem like an option.

I didn't want to do anything. I was so tired of fighting. I had no ability to see the big picture; my perspective was crowded by brokenness, bitterness, anger, and confusion. Broken from the abuse, bitter and angry at God for not saving me the way that I wanted Him to. Thinking maybe this God wasn't who I thought He was. I just wanted the nightmare to end and He wouldn't help me. All I wanted was to go home and start over.

My emotions were a constant roller coaster of riding high

knowing in my heart that this was God's way of saving me and being grateful, to plunging down the steep hill of, "Are you kidding me right now? Why *this* way? This makes no sense. and it certainly doesn't seem fair!"

Thankfully, my heart was grounded deep enough in the Truth, even if it had been masked for a while, that I could say turning my back on God completely was something I knew I never wanted to do. However, He and I had many knock-down, drag-out talks where I certainly let Him know how I felt!

It was through these raw and honest conversations that began a process I never could have even planned. I began my journey of totally falling in love with my Creator. Falling back into a deeper love for Him, learning to trust again, and with Him by my side, hearing that this "man" was saying, "I love you" and He meant it with all His heart. He taught me what love meant again.

It was not an overnight process, and even once I started to trust, I had and *still* have days when I struggle with my belief and keeping my focus on the bigger picture of God's plan. However, the still, small voice keeps telling me, "Child, trust Me. I am strong where you are weak."

God met me right in the middle of my weakest moments, right in my heart, that if placed on a monitor, would have barely been making any noise. He brought me back to life in His way. There was nothing left of the Jessica that I knew but that was okay now, because I am being created into the Jessica that God had intended me to be from the beginning. He was creating in me a new life with a new passion. A mission of service and humility, changing the world God's way instead of the way I had intended to before.

At this point, I don't know what the specifics are, as they have not been revealed to me yet, but my daily goal is to make myself available to God for Him to use me in *this* place.

I have come to learn that there can be victory prior to complete fruition of dreams. There is preparation and restoration before the sunrise and the mountaintop. That you can find peace not by the place you are, but by chasing after your God-given purpose. Prison is a dark place, but when you have the light of God shining inside you it can never be that dark.

I have been blessed with so many wonderful people to support me, and they always seem to show up at just the right time. I have developed closer relationships with many friends and family, and even developed relation-

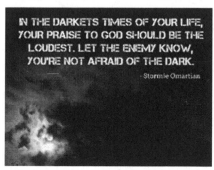

ships with people I did not know prior to this time in my life.

As far as redemption goes, I don't have my full circle yet, but I know it's coming. That the victory will be far greater than any suffering I had to endure. My mind-set prior to this experience was similar to a sports game— that there is no victory until the game is over. I will still have that final-whistle victory, but now I believe moreso in the "smaller" victories that happen prior to the end of the game: the successful play, the yards gained, and the foul shots earned.

For me, these have come in the form of God bringing people back into my life and restoring relationships, creating a stronger bond between me and my family than I ever could have imagined. Learning to love deeper than I ever had before, and having my faith expanded to realms I never thought possible.

The best part of that is being able to witness family members and friends learning to rely on the same love, that same trust and faith in God that is getting me through. They have witnessed the literal transformation of my thoughts, from belief that my life was essentially over, especially the prospect of ever having that white-picket fence family dream; I believed there was too much chaos for anyone to ever want to deal with. To now believing that God is taking a man through a journey of his own right now and preparing him for a future relationship with me. One in which he accepts and loves me *for* what has happened and who I have become as a result of having victory over it all!

> 'the PAIN that you've been feeling can't compare to the JOY that's coming. —Romans 8:18

My life now is one of hope and anticipation. The days that are a struggle still do happen, as I believe they do in any situation, where the devil tries to convince me that God is not going to work this out for the good. He likes to tell me that I have messed things up too badly for anything that I have dreamed about to come true. I am still on the jouney, that will take me to the rest of my life on this earth I believe, of finding out who God really is.

My dreams and goals seem to be the same, they have just been altered a bit to fit the story God has now made for me. I am still going to make a difference, but it will be the way God sees a need for now in the world, living out Jesus' legacy of spreading love and truth to all people.

For those of you who may be experiencing your own "Now What?" moment, just remember that God did not want this to happen, and He understands your pain because Jesus experienced all the same hearthaches here on earth. I can promise you that He will use it for His glory and your victory.

If you already know God or are still new and unsure of who He really is, know that in trusting Him you are in for so much more than you could ever have imagined, and He will create in you a person with a passion that you never dreamed you could have. It won't be all happy  moments, and God is going to dig into your heart and soul deeper than you probably ever have. He is doing this to heal you and restore you from the brokenness that the world has caused.

The Lord is your lifeline. Hold on to Him, and He will restore you to a more whole and complete person that you ever could have imagined. I know this because He is doing it for me. God has completely stolen my heart, I am in the grip of His grace. I have more purpose than I have ever had before, and it stands as proof to what the power of God combined with His grace and mercy overflowing looks like when attached to a willing spirit.

I have not yet seen all that God has in store. My story is

still being written, but I am confident that the Lord's perfect timing in this will bring about the biggest testimony my life has seen to this point.

God bless you reading this, and I pray that by the end of this book you are as confident as I am in the power and ability God has to redeem and restore anything for those who love Him.

True Freedom

At the time of writing this, Jessica still has at least two years of her sentence to serve. I will go visit her at the end of this week, and I know I will be blessed once again by the wisdom, maturity, and peace that she has. Her faith stretches me.

She is at peace in the knowledge that God is going to bring her out of there when the time is right, and in the meantime, there is obvoiusly a reason He is keeping her there. Her heart is completely open and willing to be used to love on and minister to anyone He would bring to her in there. She knows that when she gets out, her story will be able to touch many more lives.

With nothing but time to think, she has come to see the poor decisions that she made, has repented of them, and knows that this truly was the safest place she could be while her ex is still out there. She has learned the meaning of true grace and forgiveness for others. She has long since let her bitterness and anger toward her fiancé go and has taken full responsibility for her part in her actions those two years. She has learned the full meaning of the word *patience*.

She is truly one of the strongest Christ-following examples I know.

The Biggest Victory of All

Leading up to the sentencing and incarceration, Jessica told me that her mother did not really have a personal relationship with her very distant Catholic God. She did not understand how Jessica could "stand in faith" for her freedom and not take a plea bargain like everyone else. I remember being gripped by fear, thinking, *Oh no! If she didn't believe in God before, surely watching her daughter, who's leaning on God to save her, get sentenced is going to destroy any glimmer of her faith ever growing.* Isn't it funny the things we worry about? Like God couldn't handle any outcome?

At first, her mom was probably even angrier and faith-shattered than the rest of us, but it has been amazing hearing the stories from Jessica about her mom, how in her indescribable despair, she began to seek and find answers and comfort in a real, present, loving God on the other side of her prayers.

She has begun reading faith-building books and is even going to be attending a Christian retreat for families with incarcerated members. The last time I was with Jessica she said to me, "My mom could get baptized at that retreat! If me being in jail results in my mom being saved, then every single day I spent in here was worth it."

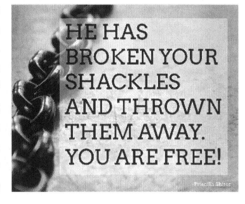

HE HAS BROKEN YOUR SHACKLES AND THROWN THEM AWAY. YOU ARE FREE!

Though currently incarcerated, I have never met a more free person than Jessica.

That's what God's full redemption and restoration looks like.

Chapter Thirteen

Abandoned but Not Alone
Susie's "Now What?" Moment

After getting married at twenty-one, dropping out of coll-
ege, and changing the direction of her career and life to support
her husband's business, Susie found herself bitter and alone at
twenty-eight. This is her story.

***

When I was a little girl, I thought I was going to be a business
woman like my dad and drive to a downtown sky-rise office. I
always thought I would get married. I did not think I would have
kids. I can't really say I thought much further than that. I'm not
really a long-term thinker. It's not like I had a huge picture or
dream for my life. I thought I would just get married and have a
fancy, corporate job.

My divorce was obviously my "Now What?" moment.

I was in my late twenties, and I remember thinking it had
ruined every single aspect of my life: Relationships with my
family, my career (because there was a part of me that blamed
being married and building our business together for not having
a "real career" or finishing my college education.), everything. A
part of me thought I would never be married again because — it
sounds silly now—but being that late in my twenties, I didn't
think I would find a guy. I thought I was going to be a poor,
single woman for the rest of my life.

I was working three jobs at the time of my divorce, so it
wasn't like I even had time for a social life. I was very angry and

bitter.

I wasn't taking any responsibility for any of it—I was a "victim"; it was all done *to* me, and I didn't have my hand in any of it.

I don't know if it was so much a moment as it was a progressive realization of, *Oh, shit. My life sucks.*

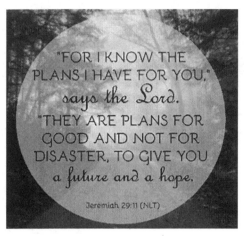

But there was a weird sense of determination, of *I'm going to get this together.* Even at my lowest point, I knew that I could do better than I was. But I kept wondering, *How did this happen? This isn't me. This doesn't happen to me.* My attitude was, *I'm just going to take control and turn this thing around.*

I told myself, *I don't need a man, or anyone, to take care of me.* I built a hard shell of protection around me, but it was actually because I was vulnerable. I wanted to put off that I was doing fine, like what had happened didn't affect me.

To say I was angry was an understatement. I was very angry, for a *very* long time. My anger was having more effect than I wanted it to have, and then I was angry that it was affecting me as much as it was!

My Turnaround

I went through some classes that I think were a step in the right direction. But I don't think my road to health really started until I met my now-husband, Keith.

There's this saying that I heard from a girl in one of my therapy classes: "Jesus with skin on." That's how I saw Keith. I feel like my healing probably could have been done another way, but I think this is how God got my attention.

When we started dating, I started going to Crossroads Church in Cincinnati with him, which was big, because during that period I really didn't attend church. I didn't even really pray. I didn't read anything for growth or restoration. I was out there on my own just trying to do it.

Getting involved in Crossroads led me to meeting new, positive influences in my life. Women who would encourage growth rather than tell me, "You're fine where you are" like my friends did at the time. There was nothing wrong with the friends I already had, but their solution was "Let's go get hammered drunk!" At times I was like, "Yes!" and other times I knew that wasn't going to get me any further.

Crossroads was a good place for me because I didn't know anybody in there, so it didn't bother me to reveal all my dirt. It was a good place for me to get it all out in a positive atmosphere, in a room of women who were only going to talk God's love back to me after I spilled out all the crap in my life. It was a chance for God to tell me the Truth—of who I am and how He feels about me, what He wants for me.

Jesus with Skin On

[I asked Susie to tell me more about how Keith helped her, how he was her "Jesus with skin on." There are lots of very unhealthy ways to use another human being or another relationship as your crutch coming out of a divorce situation. Many times if a person enters into another relationship as a means of "getting over" their ex, or even just easing that stinging pain of loneliness, it ends very badly. But Keith and Susie's relationship was different. They started as friends, with healthy boundaries, and it progressed from there.]

Keith was a real-life example of unconditional love. Since I had the baggage of my previous relationship with him—I met him because he was best friends with my ex-husband's sister—I was brutally raw and honest and transparent with him when we started hanging out. I wasn't trying to impress Keith. I didn't think he was my type at all, to be honest.

But he still pursued me, and he still loved me through my rawness, through my hardness and anger. He was very nonjudgmental. Experiencing those attributes through Keith led me to experience how Jesus actually wants us to be loved, as close as we can in human form anyway. I mean, Keith is still human.

When Keith didn't run from all the ugly, that's when I started to heal. God also showed me things through Keith about the spirit of abandonment that I didn't even know I had.

You Are Never Alone

It was also around this time that God told me to quit one of my jobs, which didn't make any sense because I needed the money. Right when I felt

> I have made you
> I will carry you
> I will sustain you
> and I will rescue you.
>
> - Isaiah 46:4

Him leading me to quit, there was something specific I wasn't going to be able to pay for if I didn't teach. I don't remember exactly what it was now, but after I made that decision to be obedient, that thing was paid for in full.

A few months later I realized I had more money saved than I ever had in my entire life, even though I had less money coming in than I did before. It was in this moment that I could see God was really taking care of me in tangible ways.

He was taking care of everything, not just money.

I never heard God audibly say, "You are not alone." But the overarching theme through that whole time in my life was He was showing me over and over I am *not* alone. He was taking care of me. At the time when I felt like no one else was.

Detours

After we were married, Keith and I were at a home meeting where a prophet from Texas came to speak. The house was packed. The prophet was walking up and down the aisles, through this parted sea of people, and he stopped along the way whenever he felt he had a word for someone. The very last person he stopped in front of was Keith, and then he started talking to both of us.

He said, "You don't know how many moving parts God had to shift around to get you two together. He had to use Christians and non-Christians to get you two to cross paths. He has way more in store for you than the two of you have even imagined. But one day in heaven, God will show you what all He had to do for you two to be together."

Hearing that gave me a whole new sense of purpose. For the first time I realized I'm here for a *reason* and God wants me to do something! He *really* is there for me. He *really* is making things happen for me. He has a place for me. And He keeps changing things based

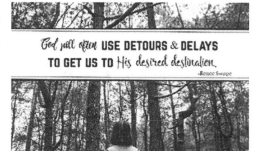

God will often USE DETOURS & DELAYS TO GET US TO *His desired destination.*
—Renee Swope

on all the decisions I was making, detours basically, to still get me to that place. That revelation changed my thoughts on God entirely.

[To be clear: Susie is *not* saying that God caused her divorce so she could be married to Keith. But I do believe He brought the two of them together after her divorce (and maybe He even tried to before her first marriage) because together they could mightily accomplish the mission He has called them to. What the devil meant for evil, God used for good.]

We all compare our relationship with God to our earthly father to some degree, and my father was very distant emotionally. So this experience broke down that barrier for me. I realized God doesn't *want* to be distant, and He's not—it was the decisions I was making throughout my life that were stiff-arming Him.

About New Dreams and Visions

I never wanted to have kids, and now I have two. When you have someone like Keith, you want to reproduce *that* into the world. So I went through the slow process of God starting to talk to me about my purpose as a mother.

After we got pregnant with Jeremy, I posted the sonogram on Facebook. A lady who works in another office of my company called me at my office and said, "I saw your sonogram on Facebook and I put my hand to the laptop and I just started praying. I'm going to mail this to you, but I'm going to read it to you now, because the Lord gave me a word about your son: 'Raise him up in the way he should go and he will not depart from it. Don't compromise your time with him. Teach him about the miracles that cement his strength. Do not give way to fear in raising him, I am giving him to you as he is Mine. My hand will always be over him in everything that comes in his life. Trust Me. Strengthen him with a strong faith that gives him his trust in Me. He will be a strong pillar in the midst of a falling world. He will stand when others fall. I trust you with this precious child of Mine.'"

As you can imagine, as I listened, I cried my eyes out. I was a mess.

So my redemption, my new vision for my life, was just realizing that part of God's mission for me was to raise up these little warriors. Maybe Satan didn't want me to have kids because he didn't want to get these world changers into the earth. Maybe there's *not* more to discover about it than that, but I don't know.

But I certainly never imagined I would be a *stay-at-home* mom!

***

It sounds really simple and trite, but God is love. And basically, the answer to all life's problems is love.

The answer to my problem with abandonment is that God loves me and He'll never leave me or forsake me, just like it says in His Word. And God loves me enough to bring a new husband, to bring a new mission, to redeem all that.

He's taken my life to places I never would have thought it would go. My life is better than I ever would have thought was possible at one point. There's just more happiness than I ever imagined. I think I take advantage of it sometimes like it's just normal and everyone experiences life like this.

I forget that I was ever married before sometimes. That I ever had to deal with any of that junk. He's taken it so far, I feel like that part of my life has been wiped clean.

What advice or words of wisdom would you have for others facing their own "Now What?" moment?

Find a person, or a group of people, who are further along spiritually than you and spend as much time around them as possible. Look for a mentor, follow the adage of "find someone who has what you want and do what they do."

Chapter Fourteen

Medically Declined
Barry's "Now What?" Moment

"Glory to God, who is able to do far beyond all that we could ask or imagine by his power at work within us."
—Ephesians 3:20

Eight months into our relationship, my boyfriend (now husband) came to me and said he wanted to pursue his lifelong dream of joining the Navy and becoming a Navy SEAL.

I laughed.

I immediately knew that was *not* the appropriate response when I watched him completely deflate in front of me and walk out of the room.

Following him, I said, "I'm sorry. I'm not laughing *at* you. Don't you even remotely see the irony in this? I just got done being married to a sailor, whom I told from the beginning I was not cut out to be a military wife, and now you want to go join the Navy."

He went on to tell me about how it had always been his dream to be a Navy SEAL. The first time he went to enlist, his dad advised him to go to college first and then join as an officer. The second time his college girlfriend gave him the ultimatum: her or the Navy, and he chose her.

Fast-forward three years and he was finally ready to go for it, so here we were having this conversation. From my past experience of handling this kind of thing the completely wrong way, I told him, "By all means, if that's your dream, go after it, with all your heart. Don't let me stop you, because if you make the decision not to go on my account, you'll only end up regretting it and hating me for it. So go, chase your dream. Don't factor me into your decision-making process. Seriously."

Here is his story from his perspective.

***

Having grown up watching my father be GI Joe once a month as an Ohio Army National Guard Reservist, I always knew one day I would follow in his footsteps and join the military. I knew it would be the way I would make my family and other people in my life proud of me. To stand. To fight. To have the honor of serving. It wasn't even a question in my mind.

A couple years after the relationship with the girlfriend who gave me the ultimatum ended, a move to a new city, and two stints as a desk jockey, I was ready for a change. I had been unhappy at my job for months; I was frustrated with bosses, politics, and my own misunderstandings of how to succeed in sales. I was mentally checked out.

I began to physically condition myself as that first dream crept back in. I even found a guy in my office who had been down this path before and was encouraging and willing to help when and where possible. Everything was lining up.

Then it all came to a screeching halt.

As I was training, I felt my legs tightening up every time I ran. Not quite like cramping; the only way I could describe it is it felt like someone stuck a ball pump in my shins and pumped them up. I went to the doctor and was told I had something called Acute Compartment Syndrome, likely from playing soccer my entire life.

The doctor explained to me that the muscles inside our legs are held in a sheath, called fascia, and essentially, the muscle in my legs had grown too big too fast for the fascia that encased them. So every time I ran it would swell and cut off blood flow to the muscles. It can actually be quite dangerous leading to muscle decay and loss and even amputation if not treated. So basically, my muscles were too big.

The doctor took a pressure gauge reading of my legs just like you would a tire. The normal pressure reading should be like a 7; my legs were a 22. He scheduled my double fasciotomy surgery immediately. I was told that after the surgery and some rehabilitation work, I would be good to go and could finally fulfill my dream.

I had the surgery. I spent about eight weeks recovering; then it was time to rehab and get serious. I left the company I was selling for. I was bartending to make money, training hard, and in my mind, I was 100 percent ready. I had read multiple books and watched every documentary I could find on Navy SEALs. I had studied the entire training and qualification process; I knew every one of the steps and schools it would take to get there.

My plan was at the six-month mark, after plenty of time to rehabilitate my legs and revamp my conditioning, we would submit paper work and move forward from there.

When the six-month wait was over, I got with the recruiter and put my packet together. I had already taken the standard ASVAB test - this was the health packet I was filling out to send to MEPS (Military Entrance Processing Station) – which included a signed release from the doctor saying surgery was a success and the issue had been addressed with zero side effects. The envelope was stamped and on the way.

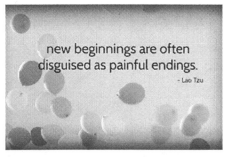
new beginnings are often disguised as painful endings.
- Lao Tzu

I can tell you exactly where I was when my phone rang a couple weeks later. I was at Rachel's parents' farmhouse. I saw the caller ID and stepped outside. Not knowing what I would do when receiving this news, I thought it best to be alone.

Then I heard, "Your application has been rejected; you've been medically declined." The reason: The doctor had written the words *exercise-induced* when describing the cause of the condition. Those two words crumbled my dream.

That conversation with the recruiter was not my finest moment. Let's just say I was glad I was outside on a farm.

> WHEN ONE DOOR CLOSES, ANOTHER OPENS; BUT WE OFTEN LOOK SO LONG AND SO REGRETFULLY UPON THE CLOSED DOOR THAT WE DO NOT SEE THE ONE WHICH HAS OPENED FOR US.
> - Alexander Graham Bell

The recruiter and I decided that he would submit an appeal to the branch-specific doctors in an attempt to have them overrule the MEPS doctors' assessment, so there was still hope. I felt confident this would go through and all would be well.

A week later I got another phone call from the recruiter. I was denied again. Same reasoning, same answer, same sadness.

That phone call was my "Now What?" moment. I was crushed. To finally commit to making this dream a reality and to have it taken away, not because of my performance, qualification, or abilities, but because of two words and someone's opinion, was devastating.

I would have gladly taken an opportunity to prove to any of the doctors I was not only fully functional post-surgery but excelling. However, after a couple more conversations with the recruiter, he expressed to me that all options had been exhausted. I would not have this opportunity.

I was completely and utterly lost.

If being in the military wasn't my purpose in life, what I was called and created to do, then what was? Who would ever respect me now? I would have to spend the rest of my life explaining to people that I had wanted to serve, but they wouldn't let me. These questions led to the next phase of my "Now What?" moment: doubt.

I hit an even lower place when I began to doubt my actual level of intent and second-guessed myself completely. If I couldn't see my biggest dream through, and so readily accepted *no* as an answer, did I really want it that badly? Could I see *anything* through? I felt like a quitter.

I saw myself as a failure. I wondered if I had failed God and His plan for my life. Had I failed my friends and family who knew the goals I was pursuing? Had I failed myself and given up without a fight? Had I procrastinated in pursuing God's plan for me and disobeyed Him to the point that I squandered away the chance to pursue my dream?

I had and still have internal conversations with myself and with God on this. And sometimes those remnants of doubt about my true desire and my worth creep back in. I think it will always be a "what if?" but I take solace in knowing that I did at least try.

While I longed to still make it happen *somehow*, I slowly developed a peace being okay with moving on from that dream. Gradually, the self-doubt and pity were fading, and God was making it possible for me to rebuild. It was not a massive "ah-ha" moment, but a series of small things.

I would catch something here or there in a conversation, on the news, on a website telling someone else's story or experience that made me feel less alone. I learned many others have had dreams and goals taken away due to all sorts circumstances outside of their control, and that they found new goals and new dreams to pursue.

During this rebuilding journey, God brought men into my life who could give me an objective opinion. They saw the potential and the best in me and slowly helped me grow and rebuild into a better person, a stronger person, than before.

It took time, but I began to see myself how they saw me. They saw what I was capable of and what I could accomplish and began to speak those things into me. I am still a work in progress. But I am pursing greatness, and I'm on a journey of finding that adventure I've always sought, just in other ways now. I still don't have a crystal-clear picture of what that looks like, but I am trusting God's leading and am following Him one step at a time. I have faith in Him to provide it all.

He taught me and reminds me over and over that everything is going to be okay. He tells me, "It will be *better* than you could have imagined. Trust me and you will see."

The biggest breakthrough is when He gave me the revelation that I will still be able to earn the respect of others, even outside the military.

> God's plans will always be bigger and more beautiful than all your disappointments.

(I know it won't be exactly the same way. All those who serve deserve a very specific, honorable, and distinguished respect that is only earned one way, and it cannot be substituted. It is those men and women who have given me the opportunity to live in a country that is full of greatness, adventure, and opportunity to be successful, earn respect, and leave a legacy of my own.)

However, this revelation took hold over time, as I started to see the men God brought into my life who weren't military, but were men who, not only I respected, but many others did as well. They encompassed all sorts of backgrounds and stories, but they were each heroes in their own way – to their families, to their communities, to their country. I was able to see that you can make an impact and earn respect in other ways. And that there are alternative methods in fighting for and preserving the freedoms in our country, right here at home.

Grace Means Grace

Early during this journey, one of the men walking with me once looked at me and said, "God told me I'm supposed to tell you that grace means grace." At the time, I actually had no idea what he was talking about, and to be truthful, I was a little creeped out. But later this wisdom became very important to my understanding and personal relationship with God.

I not only learned about God's grace as most people traditionally understand it, as forgiveness and acceptance. But I learned that one definition of *grace* is "God's empowering presence." Another is "God's active power working in and through us."

The Old Testament uses the word *chen* (adj. *chanun*), from the root *chanan*. The noun may denote "gracefulness" or "beauty," but most generally means "favor or good-will." The Old Testament repeatedly speaks of finding favor in the eyes of God or of man. The favor so found carries with it the bestowal of favors or blessings. This means that grace is not an abstract quality but is an active, working principle, manifesting itself in beneficent acts. The fundamental idea is that the blessings graciously bestowed are *freely* given, and not in consideration of any claim or merit.[39]

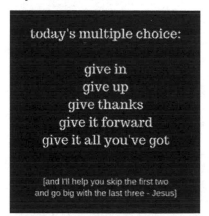

today's multiple choice:

give in
give up
give thanks
give it forward
give it all you've got

[and I'll help you skip the first two
and go big with the last three - Jesus]

This is something that I'm still working to fully grasp and accept, that God's grace covers all. God can make *anything* possible. No matter the path, God can make my life great! He can still *empower* me and put me into a role that I can excel in and say, *in no way did I earn or deserve this, and without God this wouldn't be possible. It is because of God's grace that I was able to bounce back, find a course, and pursue a new calling!*

What advice or words of wisdom would you have for others facing their own "Now What?" moment?

It can suck, bad.

So my advice is: be willing to go after something; put everything into it and don't be afraid. This could be a dream to follow, a business to start, or a relationship to pursue. Make it happen, and if you have that "Now What?" moment, know that you are not the only person who has had a moment like this. Others have, and more will in the future. But also, others have pushed forward, moved on, moved up, succeeded, dreamed, loved, and failed again. Do not be afraid. Grace means grace.

***

Barry's story is still very much being written. But the days of depression, feeling lost, and experiencing relentless mental ping-ponging are over. He went through a rough couple of years in the *blah* phase before he decided to turn that battle over and seek God for his adventure! He was even leery about sharing his story because he wondered if the fact that it is still so unfinished would keep it from being able to help anyone. But I wanted to tell you his story because I believe you need to know that your new dream will not always be born overnight, and sometimes you will linger in that in-between phase. It's not a very fun place to be, I know. But I promise you when you come out on the other side, after a while, you will forget about that time.

UNTIL GOD OPENS THE NEXT DOOR, LET'S PRAISE HIM IN THE HALLWAY

It's like women who have had a baby, and then, after nine months of discomfort and all the excruciating pain of labor, decide to do it again. The horror of that time is overshadowed by the goodness and the glory of watching their child grow and learn and experience life. Ask any woman who's given birth, and most of them will tell you they literally *can't* remember how bad it was.

The labor of birthing a new dream takes time and is painful, but it is *so* worth it.

How do you stay happy in the meantime, while that new dream is being birthed or coming to fruition? Being thankful. That's the only way you can. When you are thankful for what is to come, because you know and believe it's going to be better than what was before, you can wait in grateful anticipation.

For Barry, even though we are still walking this journey and trying to figure out what his life of purpose looks like, each day is a day of exciting possibilities!

Chapter Fifteen

Negative Prognosis
My Mom's "Now What?" Story

When she was thirty-one, my mom was diagnosed with Lupus.

Lupus is an inflammatory disease that is caused when the immune system attacks its own tissues. It's a chronic, autoimmune disease that can damage any part of the body (skin, joints, and organs). *Chronic* means that the signs and symptoms tend to last longer than six weeks and often go on for many years.

Lupus damages your immune system, which is the part of the body that fights off viruses, bacteria, and germs ("foreign invaders," like the flu). Normally our immune system produces proteins called antibodies that protect the body from these invaders. *Autoimmune* means your immune system cannot tell the difference between these foreign invaders and your body's healthy tissues and creates autoantibodies that attack and destroy healthy tissue. These autoantibodies cause inflammation, pain, and damage to various parts of the body.

I had to google all that information because I had no idea what the symptoms of Lupus were. In fact, if you met my mother, you would have no idea that she had such a potentially crippling monster lurking in her DNA.

It wasn't until I started writing this book and talking about her story to other people that I realized how even more incredible my mom is.

I asked her if she would tell her story.

***

When I was first diagnosed, the kids were young. Rachel was two and her brother, John, was six. I started losing strength in my wrists at first, and our family doctor diagnosed it as carpel tunnel so he gave me wrist braces to wear. Then it progressed from my wrists to my knees. If I sat cross-legged on the floor, I was unable to get up by myself; my husband, Donald, would have to pull me up. I told the doctor, "If it's carpel tunnel, it's everywhere!"

I had been going to the doctor regularly following a fairly serious surgery I had had a couple years earlier. They ran an arthritis profile and found I had Lupus.

I was very fortunate it was diagnosed so early. Some people go years and years, having several other misdiagnoses, before their lupus is identified because it can appear with the same symptoms of many other things.

I remember crying, just breaking down after receiving the news. I went home and read all I could on the disease (pre-computer). I knew that it would make my liver and kidneys fail. I actually thought my life would be over in a short time. I wrote out a will and cried a lot!

I was constantly tired. I lost weight and got down to 108 pounds, which is very skinny for someone who is five foot eight.

It was during this time my faith really developed. I can't say I was ever angry with God, but this event made me turn to Him for help and for peace, for the first time in my life, really. I didn't have much of a personal relationship with Him before then. But I don't think I would have known to do that if I hadn't had a first-hand account of an incredible woman of faith in my sister-in-law, Joyce.

Shortly after Donald and I were married, his sister was diagnosed with breast cancer—she was also thirty-one. She opted not to have chemotherapy and went through some organic treatments up in Ohio. While she was undergoing treatment, her husband died of a massive heart attack. [Talk about a "Now What?" Moment!] Joyce's kids were still young at the time; Danny was five or six, and Angie was only eleven or twelve.

Donald and I moved from our home in Lexington to Dry Ridge, Kentucky to help take care of Joyce and the kids. We moved on Easter Sunday in 1979. I was angry and rebellious—angry that he was moving me across the state to this little country town and into this strange woman's home. I was still young and selfish in my ways. But God used me anyway, to be there for children whose mother was so ill and to take on the responsibility of raising these children.

Joyce had only been given a month to live. She was fairly mobile at first, but toward the end she was bedridden. She died that October.

SHE DOES NOT FEAR BAD NEWS; SHE CONFIDENTLY **TRUSTS** THE LORD TO CARE FOR HER.

Psalm 112:7 (NLT)

Joyce was absolutely the most outstanding woman I have ever met. She never complained. She spent time with her children as best she could. She had her hospital bed put in the living room where she could be with them as they watched TV and played. Despite what she was going through, Joyce's spirit was always joyful. Her countenance never changed. My mother-in-law would come over every day and bathe her; she was also an incredible example of a woman of strength!

While she could still walk, Joyce asked to get up in front of our church congregation to give her testimony. They dedicated one entire Sunday evening service to it. She talked about how life on this earth is short, and you need to love God and devote all your life and your time to Him. She talked about His love for her and us.

I had never seen anyone die before. The last thing she said was she hoped Danny had a sweater on as he was riding his bicycle in the basement. She took a breath and never took another. Most of the family was there, as they had been for many days in the evenings when they got off work.

When I received my diagnosis of Lupus, it was a shock of irony to realize I was the same age Joyce had been when she died!

I went every three months to the doctor. They drew blood, I peed in the cup, and thankfully I never got any worse. I actually regained my strength over time; however, because of the medication, I began putting on weight (thirty pounds in a very short time) and I developed the "steroid chipmunk face." (I believe God works on your vanity too!)

But I was able to raise my own children.

And after a while, when it didn't get any worse, I decided to make the best of it. I decided to live my life just like I would have before I knew about the disease. With the medications I was taking, I wasn't supposed to get stressed out (HA! Try raising two teenagers!), I wasn't supposed to do a lot of manual labor, and I wasn't supposed to have much exposure to the sun. But playing in the dirt was my passion. When the kids

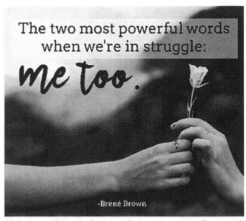

The two most powerful words when we're in struggle: me too.

-Brené Brown

were young enough, I would put them down for naps and sneak outside to work in my garden or flower bed. Eventually I even started and ran my own greenhouse for a decade! I wasn't very good at following the restrictions.

The biggest blessing in all of this is now being able to help other people in our church or community. When someone comes forward who's been diagnosed with Lupus, I can say, "I've been there, I know what you're going through. But you can handle it. You can live a full life just like normal even with it." And it really gives them hope.

Through it all, God was with me. He gave me the right doctors, and I was where I needed to be at the right time. My faith was increased exponentially. And now I know whatever I may face in this life, He is right there with me the whole time. He is so good.

Chapter Sixteen

Paralyzed
Terri's "Now What?" Story

"Some life circumstances are not meant to be understood; the call is just to keep moving forward one step at a time. That's called faith." My name is Terri Nida. I wrote that on my Facebook page a few days before I broke my neck.

On August 18, 2013, I suddenly felt dizzy. It had been a nice Sunday afternoon. The hanging plants on my balcony were slowly swinging in the breeze, and I remember admiring them. I remember what I was wearing: a mauve-colored peasant blouse and white pedal-pusher pants. I remember that the sun was shining through the dining room windows and my cats were curled up on the couch. It had been a good day, because I had spent the day in prayer and I fasted for eight hours that day. Only eight hours. I had fasted several times before, for more than twenty-four hours on a few occasions, and never had a problem. This day was different.

"I have been asked hundreds of times in my life why God allows tragedy and suffering. I have to confess that I do not know the answer. I have to accept, by faith, that God is sovereign, and that He is a God of love and mercy and compassion in the midst of suffering."

— Billy Graham

What was the purpose of my fast? I felt disconnected from God and disconnected from people. I prayed an earnest prayer for God to do whatever He needed to do to help me to reconnect with Him. You see, about twenty years earlier I had been a devoted follower of Christ. I had even picked up my life in North

Carolina and moved it to Washington, DC, to be part of a church planting. I remember my faith soaring at that time, and I was an eager witness to others about Christ. But somewhere along my journey I became disillusioned through the death of my mother and failed relationships. I became a legalistic Christian and lived a life of drudgery. I eventually turned myself back over to the world and all its enticing lies about where happiness comes from.

It had been a long time since I felt my faith soar like those earlier days. So rising up off my knees on that beautiful, sunny August day left me feeling an incredible resolve. I remember how free I felt. I remember how much lighter I felt. And that's when I decided to break my fast and eat. I simply went to the refrigerator, and the dizziness hit me. The next time I opened my eyes my view of the world, my attitude toward God and people, and the things I treasured most in my life, were forever altered.

When I opened my eyes, my whole body was tingling. Nothing below my shoulders moved, no matter how hard I tried. All I could see was ceiling tiles, and I felt completely disoriented. I was still able to move my head, and I tried to turn my head to get oriented. I remember almost passing out during that head turn because the pain was so excruciating.

Somewhere between the refrigerator and the floor, I had fallen backward and probably hit the stove handle just right to snap the C4 vertebrae in my neck.

I knew I was paralyzed. I remember thinking to myself, *Okay, this is how it is.* I was in and out of consciousness for the next day and a half. When I was awake, I spent time praying and reciting scriptures that I had memorized for challenging life moments. Although I never expected a life moment like this one. And please don't think I'm a spiritual giant. I was terrified, and this was all I knew to do.

My coworker came the morning of the second day with the

police. The door was broken down, and I was found lying on the kitchen floor. Close to death.

I had just returned from a vacation in Cancun a few months earlier and had kept up my tan via the tanning bed. My hair was streaked with blonde from being in the Mexican sunshine and $200 highlights at the salon. I worked out. I took walks. I had been athletic most of my life, so I was fit and muscular. I had a closet full of clothes, an apartment full of new furniture, a new car, many friends, and a close-knit family.

I seemed to have it all together on the outside, but inside I was groaning. I felt a yearning that could not be satisfied.

> Sometimes God lets you hit rock bottom so that you will discover that He is the ROCK at the bottom.
>
> - Dr. Tony Evans

Unbeknownst to the world, I was at the bottom of a dark spiritual well and didn't know how to climb out. And I wouldn't ask for help. Little did I know I was getting ready to take a journey with God that would teach me how to claw out of that well, inch by inch.

When I woke up in the ICU a few days later, I suddenly had a desperate need for support from friends and family and a relationship with God. Thus I began my journey of physical, spiritual, and emotional healing.

After a long hospitalization, I went to live in a nursing facility. My family members didn't feel they could provide adequate care so this was the only alternative. After having such a carefree, independent, active lifestyle, I was suddenly completely dependent on the nursing staff to live.

Prior to the accident I was on only one medication. Now I have to swallow twenty pills throughout the day. The staff are responsible for everything. They take care of my hygiene. They dress me. They exercise me. They lift me in something like a human forklift to put me in my wheelchair. For some reason it makes me feel humiliated to be lifted in that thing. To this day I still hate it. Then they put me to bed at night. But somehow I have kept my faith. Some days I'm holding on by two fingernails and a thread, but I somehow hold on.

Since I became a quadriplegic, I've kept the belief that God has a greater purpose in this than what I can see. I believe this with all my heart! And yet as I maneuver through an odyssey of emotions as I face increased medical problems and visits to the hospital ICU, it's been hard for me not to think of each day as a negative event.

I find myself asking God, "Can we skip all these days of suffering and just get to the end product?" I get the big picture in all this, but the day-to-day pieces allude me. Losing the things I thought made up my identity—my home, my job, my physical appearance, all of my material possessions—was an adjustment I was not prepared to face. And learning to live life in a facility with twenty-four-hour dependence on others was frustrating, degrading at times, and very discouraging.

In the first year I allowed myself to believe that maybe God had deserted me. In fact, I had some devastating things happen during that time and found myself asking God, "What good is all of this?" I was bitter and filled with rage much of the time. I was angry at God and angry at people. I lashed out at the nursing facility staff, and I lashed out at my family. I was confused, paranoid, and deeply depressed.

peace.
it does not mean to be in a place where there is no noise, trouble or hard work. It means to be in the midst of those things and still **be calm in your heart.**

(unknown)

Thanks to modern technology, in this second year I've been able to diligently study the Bible, write a blog about my life, and get input from other trusted Christian women. And of course I pray. But my prayers are so different now. They are raw and real and searching for answers. As a result, I feel like I've gained some positive perspective on my quadriplegia.

Don't get me wrong—I haven't had a day yet when I felt happy about my current life circumstances. There are days when I just want to give up and wish I could disappear from this earth. In all honesty, I think there will be many more days like that ahead. But I do believe this life has a purpose, if I can just live victoriously one day at a time.

I talked with a dear friend of almost thirty years recently about healing. She is someone I consider to be a spiritual mentor. She taught me about healing and how it comes to us in different ways. I realized when I was able-bodied I looked for self-worth through things of this world, and I never felt at peace or complete. Now that I have none of these things I am completely reliant on God for my peace and sense of completeness. This has been and continues to be a very healing process, and it has only come to me as a result of my accident.

On a good day, I think, *Maybe I've been put here to be a light. Maybe some of these people just need me to smile at them each day and give them some hope. Maybe they need an advocate, especially the ones who can't even speak.*

***

I love that last line. I tear up at the unbelievable selflessness in it.

Terri is not only making an impact on the world she's physically living in but her blogs[40] are helping hundreds of people all around the world. Her rawness and vulnerability in sharing the very real emotional struggles and spiritual battles she faces every day, backed up by the light of Scripture, are an inspiration to so many!

I remember the first time I stumbled across her blog it literally took my breath away. What an amazing pillar of faith in our world! Her story challenges me and makes me reevaluate my own first-world problems. Every one of her posts strengthens my faith.

From the outside, I can clearly see how God's hand is moving in her life, how He dwells in and with her, even on the days she struggles to see it herself. I guess we are all that way sometimes; other people can see the work God is doing through us before we can.

Terri and I have had many lengthy, thoughtful discussions

about her accident and her present circumstances, and I want to clarify some things to avoid any confusion you may have. This is a difficult subject to navigate and has been very twisted and perverted by the church over the course of history.

Neither Terri nor I believe that God *caused* her accident to happen. Not as any sort of test or a trial, as some may claim. Nor was she being punished by God for turning away from Him for so long, as those legalistic *religious* people might tell her. Neither was her prayer for closeness with Him that day answered with quadriplegia as a sadistic "be careful what you wish for" type of menace. That is *not* the way our loving God works. Remember 3 John 1:2: "Beloved, I wish above all things that thou may prosper and be in health, even as thy soul prospers." I don't really count quadriplegia on the prosperity and health side of the spectrum.

I personally believe that since she was praying for *more* of God, her enemy was eager to thwart that request. I believe God had a big plan to use Terri's life in a big way (and still does), but the bigger threat you pose to your enemy, the sooner and stronger he's going to come after you. What better way than to take everything in Terri's entire life away in order to provoke her? To try and cause her to turn against the very One she was seeking? To curse God and die, just like that same enemy tried to get Job to do four thousand years ago?

If you've never read Job's book of the Bible, I recommend it. RECAP: Job was the most faithful man on earth in his time, and because of that, he was abundantly wealthy and blessed in every way. Satan came to challenge God: "Let me test Your servant Job. He's only faithful because You have blessed him so much. I bet if I took all those things away, he would turn against You" (my paraphrase). So God *allowed* Satan to destroy Job's entire world: his crops, his livestock, his health, his family. He *allowed* all that happen to Job so He could prove to the devil that His servant truly was faithful. That despite his circumstances, no matter what Satan threw at him, Job would never turn against the One who gave it all to him in the first place.

At the end of his story, God restored *everything* to Job—*twice as much* as he had before the trials! Not only was he more spiritually rich and mature, he was fully restored and richer in every *physical* way as well.

Terri agrees her story is very much like Job's in that, even though God did not *cause* this thing to happen to her, He did *allow* it. Why? That's an answer we might not get this side of heaven.

But despite what was meant for evil, God is able to use for His good. He is developing in Terri a fulfilling new vision and purpose. She is a gifted writer and is passionate about sharing her story. God is using her as a powerful testimony to His goodness despite the brokenness of her body and this world. And now she has a bigger platform from which to share it. "And we know that all things work together for good to them that love God, to them who are the called according to his purpose" (Romans 8:28). What a slap in the face to the devil that is!

Finally, God has also answered the very prayer she uttered that day. She is walking closer to Him now than she ever imagined she would before her fall!

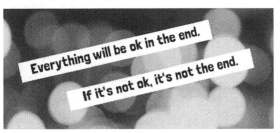

And while my selfish heart wants the rest of her double portion to look like healing and wholeness physically mani-fested here on this earth, I am patiently contented to watch her spirit and soul being healed for now. To watch her being used as an instrument of His glory and faithfulness. I don't know what God has planned for her future, but I know it's good. I also know He is with her every step of the way, and I know everything will be made right in the end.

Chapter Seventeen

Survivor
Josh's "Now What?" Story

*"From the night which covers me, as dark as shadow of
the darkest abyss, with only a blanket of stars to guide my way,
I thank God for my unconquerable soul. In the fell clutch of
chance and circumstance I have not winced nor cried aloud.
Bludgeoned by both chance and circumstance my head
is bloody, yet unbowed and beyond this place, past the tears
and brokenness and all my despair, is my rebirth and beginning
life anew. The past is behind me and if that or other demons shall
menace me, they'll find me unafraid."*
—Josh Cooper

To say Josh's childhood was dysfunctional would be the understatement of the century. His mother walked out when he was just fifteen months old, leaving him home alone while his father was at work. She came back a few weeks later and kidnapped him, only to spend the next seventeen years verbally and physically abusing him. All that happened after she attempted to take his life. While pregnant with Josh, his mother had an abortion. But Josh survived.

Did you know that was even possible? Because I sure didn't, not until the first time I heard his story.

Since then, I've learned there is an entire group of people living today whose parents tried to have them murdered in the womb, but they did not die. They are abortion survivors.

There are a couple "types" of abortion survivors:

1. Twin abortion survivors: These are people whose parents

didn't realize they were having twins, so their twin was aborted but they survived. (I found this was actually fairly common.)

2. Attempted abortion survivors: These are people who survived an actual abortion attempt. In other words, the abortion failed to kill them.

Most of the time the attempted abortion induces labor and the babies are born prematurely. Many die shortly after birth due to medical conditions and complications caused by the abortion itself; some live but with varying degrees of deformities or disabilities. And then you have the horror stories about men like Kermit Gosnell, who would sever the spinal cords of babies born alive after a failed abortion. But there are also many people who are walking, breathing, and living right next to you, and you may never know that was the way their life began.

In my research, I learned that statistics are far from comprehensive for abortion survivals in the United States. The number of abortions alone, including the babies' ages, is not always accurately reported, so the difficulty in determining the incidence of survivors is not surprising.

Rough estimates—"soft" numbers—are available. But there are hard numbers that have been reported in other countries that are useful in not only analyzing the incidence of survivors there but also in tentatively generalizing these findings for the United States.

Based on statistics from Australia, Canada, and the UK,[41] we can estimate that at a minimum there are seventy-five children who survive abortions in the United States each year.

Physical ramifications aside, a human being's most basic emotional need is to feel wanted, accepted, and loved. Can you imagine living with the knowledge that you weren't wanted to the extent that someone tried to have you killed before you even took your first breath? And that someone was the person who should love and care about you most!

Josh has to live with that knowledge every day. Let him tell you his story.

***

For what it's worth, I think I was a pretty happy kid, and no matter how dark the world around me grew, I couldn't shake this feeling I had that I was special, unique in some way I couldn't quite describe. I had always felt as if I was meant for something more, something greater than myself.

My dad told me that when he and my mom got married, they tried to get pregnant right away. Since my mom already had my step-brother, she didn't really want have any more kids, but my dad really wanted a child of his own, so they kept trying.

A year later she got pregnant. My dad says that my mother became increasingly hard to live with. She would get angry and sometimes throw herself down on our steps and slide down on her belly in attempt to "get even" with him and to cause some irreparable harm to me. Once she even got so angry she began beating her stomach in attempt to kill me. These outbursts would break my dad's heart and drive him to tears or sometimes unparalleled fits of anger.

Not exactly something you want to tell your son, but I grew up with both parents telling me how much the other didn't love me.

I secretly hoped that they were both wrong.

The truth about my mother is this:

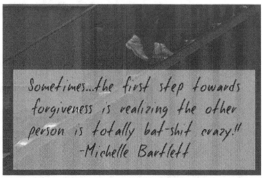

Sometimes...the first step towards forgiveness is realizing the other person is totally bat-shit crazy.!!
-Michelle Bartlett

she was the greatest actress I have ever seen, and even knowing all this, my love for her was still boundless and all I ever wanted was for her to love me in return.

There were small glimpses of love I would get, like when she would read to my brother and me, or the night she snuck in my room and tucked me in and whispered she loved me while she thought I was sleeping. These are the moments I held on to. I imagined one day I would wake up and she would apologize for everything, or say she was kidding all along and we would laugh about it together.

But more often she was yelling, accusing, punishing me, blaming me for everything, and all the while telling me how much my dad didn't want me or love me.

My dad was a wonderful man, my hero. He's the one who told me and taught me about God. Who instilled faith in me and built it up. But I only got to see him every other weekend after my parents divorced. I cherished and looked forward to those times together.

When I was nine, I fell in love with reading (in part due to the stories my mother had shared so passionately with my brother and me), and then in the fourth grade I found my real passion, which is writing. What started out as a short writing exercise turned into a fifty-page typed manuscript, with what my teacher said was excellent flow, characterization, and character growth.

All my life I had never really been praised or thought I was really good at anything, so it wasn't until I turned in this first "short" story that I received real and genuine affirmation. I fell in love with watching people read something I wrote and seeing their excitement, their wonder. When I had to read a story to my class, I would look up and see my audience hanging on to every word I said.

Writing saved me. It became my therapy. It set me free.

Whenever I thought about quitting, I would hear God say, "Try." Even when my heart was broken, or whenever I was struggling with depression, I would do my best impression of a pen and imagine every problem looked like a page.

The first time I ever felt really challenged in my dream of writing came when I was seventeen and was working on an outline to a story. My mother came up behind me and asked what I wanted to do after high school. And do you know what she said to me when I told her I wanted to be a writer? She laughed and said, "You shouldn't. Your chances are one in a million of being successful."

I said, "Maybe I'm that one."

She tried telling me I should give up on my dreams and to pursue a career where the financial success was more guaranteed. She tried telling me to give up on the one thing that I loved, the one thing that made me feel alive, and it was then I realized, I didn't care what anyone else thought, I would keep doing this for me.

Giving up on writing would never be an option, because I had all these stories, these wildfires, these characters, and all these words born inside of me, imprinted onto my very soul. And I believe God put them there.

I believe you have to follow what you're passionate about; you need to at least try and keep trying.

I just imagine if I ever gave up on writing, I would one day be on my death bed, and I would see all these characters staring crestfallen down at me. Some would be bitter, others would be heartbroken, and they would pace up and down my bedside, saying, "We came to you to give us life; we came to you so that you'd write us so that you could breathe life into us. But now we're dying without ever having a chance to live; that's all we wanted, was a chance. We came to you and you let us down, and now when you pass on, we'll be forgotten and lost forever. We'll die here with you without ever having to live."

My mother would have been just as happy to send those characters to their graves as she tried with me in her womb. But my mother was wrong. And whatever she thought she saw in me was also wrong . . . Because I *am* that one in a million, and so are you.

We all have that something special inside of us. We're born with storms, tidal waves, comets, and forest fires raging on within us; we're all born and gifted with this magic spark. As kids jumped from couch to couch because the floor was lava, and we learned to fly by tying a blanket around our shoulders. We were born capable of talking to animals and singing to birds, of seeing stories in the clouds.

I've learned that everyone has a story to tell, and their stories can only add to your own.

That conversation with my mother was far from the worst, but my "Now What?" moment came after another conversation with her just a year later, when I was eighteen.

The day I finally broke down and killed myself.

I had just graduated high school and felt like life had thrown everything including the kitchen sink at me.

It was on graduation day. After having my heart broken for the second time by this girl I loved, I came home desperate for some measure of sympathy and told my mother the whole story about her.

After pouring out my heart, she responded flatly, "I don't care, you're just a stupid, pathetic loser and I can't stand you. I never could, and the worse thing is that I never wanted you. You're nothing but a stupid mistake, and if it wasn't for your father, I would have never birthed you, he's the only reason you're still here because he wanted you. I even tried having an abortion! You were the accident that was never supposed to be and I think you would have been better off dead, because no one will ever love or want a weak, pathetic, loser like yourself."

Then she turned and walked away, striding toward her craft room, mumbling about how much she resented me and saying something about the only reason she put up with me for so long was for the child support money.

I could feel what remained of my already wounded heart crumble into a million little pieces. I was broken, in every sense of the word, and I couldn't move. Not at first, anyway. All I could do was watch her disappear into her little craft room, expecting at any moment for her to pop back out and tell me this was all some sort of twisted and cruel joke. I didn't want to think she was serious. But after several minutes, I realized she wasn't coming back. I just stood there speechless.

I hear every eighteen minutes someone commits suicide and every forty seconds someone attempts one. I was about to become another statistic.

In that moment I lost my faith. I hated God. I couldn't fathom why He would make this woman my mother and never allow me any real happiness.

I had been hopeful my entire life, wanting and trying to believe that things would get better, believing that they had to. But my battles were too numerous, too long and hard, and I was tired.

Immediately I turned, headed upstairs, and grabbed a few prescription pill bottles my mother kept in our medicine cabinet. With a bottle of Vicodin that I had left over from my wisdom teeth surgery in hand, along with the various other pills that I had stuffed into my pockets, I took one final look at my reflection in the mirror and waved good-bye to the person I used to be, the person I used to know.

Returning to my room, I closed and locked my door, filled my cd player with my favorite CDs, and took an entire bottle of prescription sleeping pills, along with about three quarters of the rest.

I wrote a single sentence on my desk's notepad, "This is my good-bye, I've waited too long, I'm not worth anything, and tell Dad I'm sorry."

It didn't take long for the room to start to spin and the shortness of breath to begin. I fell onto my bed, crawling up onto the sheets feeling so cold as my body went numb, I felt pins and needles all over. I was suffocating, struggling to breathe, then my world went black.

At first darkness was all I could see and feel. I was relieved, because I was finally free from all the pain and loneliness that had plagued me for so long. No longer did I feel all that was tearing my heart apart. It was over and death wasn't as bad I thought. I felt a strange sense of comfort in the darkness that coiled and wrapped around me.

I was a little disappointed though. I was hoping to find myself before God so I could demand an explanation, an apology for all that had been wrong. But I didn't, and I didn't see a light at the end of the tunnel or loved ones who had already passed over. Instead, I found myself in a world surrounded by utter darkness, and for a moment it was soothing and a little peaceful. But then I felt this jerk, and I had a sense I was falling.

I was falling faster and faster, what felt like cool air rushing up to greet me as I plummeted downward, feeling the air grow and become warm, then hot as it passed over me. The realization of what I had done hit me then. I had committed (what I believed to be) a cardinal sin—I had committed suicide! I wasn't going to get my trial; I wasn't going to able to curse at the God who made me and let me cry so many tears. I wasn't going to get answers, and I would never learn why or the reasons for any of it. I was going straight to Hell.

In my fear, I cried out to God, and it was then I felt the descent slow and the heat dispel, until I was once again just floating there in the inky blackness.

I felt like I was being watched, and I sensed a profound sadness in the air around me. Then what I can only describe as warm, comforting arms wrapped around me, pulling me close and lifting me up. I have no words for the feelings that washed over me. The love I sensed was overpowering, and I felt like a child in the warm, loving arms of a loved one, of a Father who was holding me close.

I began to cry as I heard the voice apologizing for the struggles I've had, saying that despite what I had done, He was still proud of me. He told me not to lose hope and that I had to stay, I had to go back. He asked me to stay strong, to have faith and to live, to really live; He assured me that I'd go on to do great things in time.

Without really thinking I felt myself letting go. I was blinded by this sudden light, and then I discovered I was outside, flying miles above the earth. Soon I saw my house come into view, and I fell into the roof and landed on my bed, crashing with a jolt into my body.

I firmly believe that I died that day. And when I woke up, I felt okay, even though I knew my worst was far from over.

I moved out. A few months later my mother and I had another argument over the phone, and that was the last time I have talked to her.

Since then, God has helped me learn you have to let go. You have to release the hurt. Otherwise it will own you forever and you'll never escape. You need to have the strength to fight back and take your life back.

The wounds can and may eventually close and scab over, becoming the very scars that make up who we are, reminding us of our journey on this crazy path called life. My scars will always be there.

But now I try and live as much for tomorrow as I can. I'm tired of looking back. So from here on, the only time I look back is to think, *Look how far I've come.* And that's what keeps me going.

My biggest lessons have been to forgive quickly, to speak calmly, to be slow to anger, and to love always.

Tell Your Story

I never realized how much I needed to talk about everything I went through growing up until I started telling my story. I was always afraid of being a burden or people accusing me of being a liar or that I would come off as a whining victim.

But despite everything I've been through, I'm still alive. I'm still standing. So that's why I blog, and that's why I share my story with you, so that you know that things do get better. Even when it feels like you've hit rock bottom, with no hope of getting out. Because you can.

It won't be easy. It'll be the hardest, longest, and toughest battle you'll ever face. You may get tired or fall along the way, which we all do, but what's important is to keep getting back up. No matter what life throws at you, you have to keep pressing forward, never stop reaching out.

Even if you lose that spark, all is not lost, believe me. *Loss sometimes marks a larger return.*

Being a writer, I often lose several pages or entire chapters that I had spent half the night working on. I have even spent an entire month of writing, honing, editing, making it perfect, only to lose it (which tends to make you want to throw your computer out the window).

But after I finish shouting to the heavens and bashing my head against my desk and pacing the floors, I take a breath and mutter a few swears and other nonsense before taking another breath. Then I crack my knuckles, sit back down, and start all over again, much like life.

Sometimes you may lose a job, a spouse, a saved file, a flash drive, or a loved one. No matter what it is you've lost, you eventually have to pull yourself back together and start over.

Which can be daunting, I know. I've had to start over and rebuild my own life a few times, and it's something that never gets any easier; it was never easy to begin with. But you do it because you have too, because quitting and giving up isn't an option.

I have survived and been through too much to have it kill me right there at the end. Besides, if I quit, I'll never know how close I came to achieving everything I set out to do.

Many may call me a failure. But to me, failing is something that only happens once you've given up. I may not have achieved much of what I set out to do and had hoped to have done by this point in my life, but I've gained more than I could have ever hoped for; I discovered that family is what you say it is, not what it should be.

Because of my dreams I learned perspective. I can see beyond and past myself and all my insecurities, and I can see a world where anything is possible. A world filled with incredible joy, happiness, and wonder. I see this world whenever I close my eyes. I see what we as a people can really do, I see our potential, and I see it in everyone.

This is why I write, because it's my dream to do so, and I believe that my dreams, along with yours, are given to us directly from the hand of God Himself. He put those dreams within us. The fruition of dreams rarely comes easy. Like all talents or gifts, they must be nurtured, given time to grow.

I still stumble here and there. I have struggled an uphill battle with depression. But I fought on and refused to give up. I didn't let the darkness encroach around my heart and soul; I didn't let it define me. Even in the times when it threatened to swallow me whole.

I've always believed in something being out there looking over me, something so much bigger than me. Because I believe in God. And I'm incredibly stubborn. I've been a survivor my whole life.

For those of you who are going through your own "Now What?" moment, I offer this advice: Don't give up; don't surrender what means the most to you. You'll be challenged, and you may find yourself fighting some of the hardest battles of your life. Life can hit pretty hard sometimes, and some blows will knock you down. Sometimes it'll feel like you may never be able to pick yourself back up or even be you again. But even if you can't see it, the struggles we face now, the pain, humiliation, they don't really last. Though it seems like it may never end, it will; just give it time and have a little faith. Learn from your mistakes. You can't be afraid of picking yourself up, dusting yourself off, and going one more round.

Remember you're not alone. I'm pulling for you. I love you and I'm here for you, always.[42]

"Now WHAT?"

Questionnaire

I would love to hear your story! You can answer the questions in true open answer form or use this questionnaire as a guideline to write your story and start to see how God can use your pain for your purpose and His glory. It takes courage and vulnerability to tell your story. But when you do, I know God will use it to help others going through similar situations by giving them hope and letting them know they are not alone. Even if you don't share it with me, I encourage you to still do this exercise.

1. What was your original vision/dream for your life? How did you think life would go?

2. What was your "Now What?" moment (the moment everything you dreamed and imagined was challenged or crushed)?

3. How did you react to your "Now What?" moment?
   a. What did you feel, think, and do?
   b. How was your faith affected? Were you angry at God? Rebellious? Hurt? Offended?
   c. How long did it last?
   d. What was the absolute lowest point?

4. How did God meet you in that place?
   a. Are there specific things He said to you?
   b. Things He showed you?

c. People He brought into your life?
d. Things He taught you?

5. How has God redeemed your story? What does life look like now?
   a. What victories have you had so far?
   b. What new dreams and visions do you have?
   c. What have you learned?

6. Do you see yet how God can use your "Now What?" moment for a bigger purpose?

7. What advice or words of wisdom would you have for others facing their own "Now What?" moment?

I would LOVE to hear your "Now What?" story!

Feel free to submit online at
www.nowwhatstory.com/now-what-questionaire
Or e-mail to: **stories@nowwhatstory.com**

Special Thanks to:

Julie Breihan – I couldn't have asked for a better editor to lovingly guide my first project. Turning over a first book (or maybe every book? I don't know yet) for editing is kind of like tearing open your soul and inviting someone to walk inside. It's exposing the most intimate parts of your inner self and trusting that person not to return pieces of you shattered and bloody. The first edited draft I got back from you, I couldn't open for 3 weeks, my stomach would curl every time I thought about redlines striking through the most vulnerable parts of myself. But for every correction or change, you included a praise, which made tweaking my thoughts easier. You took every phone call when I was freaking out about *any* part of this process, even when you didn't have the answers for me. Above all else, you encouraged me to maintain my voice first and foremost. Thank you.

All my cheerleaders who helped me hone ideas and/or contributed in any way to this project: Mamma, Gaynelle, TaLarrya, Susie (and thank you for giving me those beautiful babies I call my niece and nephews to love), Rebekah, Meagan Newell, Terri Nida, Josh Cooper, Jennifer Osborn, Carey Corp, Maria Mingo, Brian Tome, Chuck Mingo.

Brad Covey - thank you for my beautiful cover design and website – your graphic design skills and patience never cease to amaze! And thanks for being the first person to ask for my autograph! ;)

Max Henry of Max Effect - thank you for taking on my high maintenance interior layout with enthusiasm and grace.

Tami Dever of TLC Graphics – for lending me your valuable time and expertise. I love your servant's heart!

My final proofreaders - your eyes caught what mine and Julie's had gone blind to: Connie, & Mindy.

And finally to: Lysa Terkeurst, Proverbs31 Ministries, the SheSpeaks Staff, and every one of the other authors I name in this book, thank you for going before me, for your words, and for giving me the courage to use my voice to give hope to others.

References:

1. Phil Wickham, "Safe," *Heaven and Earth*, produced by Peter Kipley, Brentwood, TN, INO Records, 2009, digital download.

2. Mandisa, "He Is with You," Freedom, by Ronnie Freeman and Cindy Morgan, produced by Brown Bannister, Brentwood, TN, Sparrow Records, 2009, digital download.

3. Brian Tome, Free Book (Nashville, TN: Thomas Nelson, 2010), 205–6.

4. *Wikipedia*, s.v. "antinomianism," [accessed November 2014], https://en.wikipedia.org/wiki/Antinomianism.

5. David and Lisa Frisbie, *Happily Remarried* (Eugene, OR: Harvest House Publishers, 2005), 44–45.

6. Josh Wilson, "Before the Morning," Life Is Not a Snapshot, Brentwood, TN: Sparrow Records, 2010.

7. Lisa Bevere, Girls with Swords (Colorado Springs, CO: WaterBrook Press, 2013), 59.

8. Tome, Free Book, 165–66

9. Dr. Les and Leslie Parrott, Saving Your Marriage Before It Starts (Grand Rapids, MI: Zondervan, 2001), 14.

10. Stormie Omartian, *The Power of a Praying Wife* (Eugene, OR: Harvest House Publishers, 1997), 41.

11. http://psychcentral.com/lib/the-myth-of-the-perfect-marriage/

12. Willard Harley, Jr., *His Needs, Her Needs* (Grand Rapids, MI, Fleming H. Revell, 2001), 67.

13. Omartian, *Power of a Praying Wife*, 26.

14. Andy Stanley, *The New Rules for Love, Sex and Dating* (Grand Rapids: Zondervan, 2014), 40.

15. Vicki Santillano, "10 Things Married People Want Couples to Know Before They Commit," www.worldlifestyle.com, http://www.worldlifestyle.com/relationships/10-things-married-people-want-couples-to-know-before-they-commit.

16. Gary Chapman, *Things I Wish I'd Known Before We Got Married* (Chicago: Northfield Publishing, 2010), 23.

17. Les and Leslie Parrott, *Saving Your Marriage Before It Starts* (Grand Rapids, MI: Zondervan, 2006), 36-37, 39-40

18. Gary Chapman, *Things I Wish I'd Known Before We Got Married* (Chicago: Northfield Publishing, 2010), 18.

19. John Gottman, *The Seven Principles for Making Marriage Work* (New York: Three Rivers Press, 1999), 27.

20. http://www.dictionary.com/browse/contempt

21. http://www.dreammoods.com/dreamdictionary/e2.htm

22.   http://dreamstop.com/ex-boyfriend-girlfriend-husband-wife-dream-symbol/

23. http://m.huffpost.com/us/entry/891551.html

24.   http://www.dreamsymbolism.info/dreamdictionary/tornado-dreams.php

25. Barbara Wilson, *The Invisible Bond* (Sisters, OR: Muttnomah Publishers, 2006), 11, 13, 14.

26. Anne Morrow Lindbergh, *Gifts from the Sea* (New York: Pantheon, 1991)

27. Kay Warren, *Choose Joy Because Happiness Isn't Enough* (Grand Rapids, MI: Revell, 2013), 195

28. Lysa TerKeurst, https://www.facebook.com/OfficialLysa/photos/a.427520367693.211047.338478917693/10153336029397694

29. David and Lisa Frisbie, *Happily Remarried* (Eugene, OR:

Harvest House, 2005), 7.

30. Omartian, *Power of a Praying Wife,* 40-41

31. Les & Leslie Parrott, Saving Your Second Marriage Before It Starts (Grand Rapids, MI: Zondervan, 2001), 43.

32. Tome, *Free Book,* 164-165

33. Bill and Pam Farrell, *Men Are Like Waffles, Women Are Like Spaghetti* (Eugene, OR: Harvest House, 2001), 209, 212.

34. https://www.facebook.com/officiallysa

35. *Merriam-Webster,* s.v. *restore,* http://www.merriam-webster.com/dictionary/restore

36. Andy Stanley, *The New Rules for Love, Sex and Dating* (Grand Rapids, MI: Zondervan, 2014), 9.

37. https://crossroads.net/thedaily

38. Gary Newell, "A Fighting Spirit", Raleigh, NC, Leadership Team Development, 2010

39. http://www.bible-researcher.com/grace.html

40. https://diaryofaquadriplegic.wordpress.com/

41. http://www.nationalrighttolifenews.org/news/2013/04/awareness-is-growing-about-abortion-survivors/#.VRH4QOEerP8

42. Excerpts taken from http://authorjcooper.com/?s=scars with permission from author.

45367989R00174

Made in the USA
Middletown, DE
02 July 2017